# MIRROR OF MY SOUL, SANCTUM OF MY HEART

Jasmina Agrillo Scherr

Book design by Jasmina Agrillo Scherr

Cover design by Ramajon
Bikeapelli Press, LLC

Jasmina's Books are available for order through
Ingram Press Catalogues

In writing this memoir, I have tried to recreate events, locales and conversations from my understanding and memories of them. If anyone is offended by anything I have said it is purely unintentional. In order to maintain their anonymity in some instances I have changed the names of individuals.

Jasmina Agrillo Scherr

Visit my website at jasminasbooks.com

Printed in the United States of America

First Printing 2015
By
Sojourn Publishing, LLC

ISBN: 978-1-62747-015-5

Ebook ISBN: 978-1-62747-016-2

LCN: Pending

# Dedication

*T*his memoir is dedicated to my grandfather, Charles Nuncio Agrillo 1906-1987. You were a quiet, simple, humble, wise spiritual master in disguise who taught me that miracles are born of love and conviction, that my mind which created the diseased condition can heal the condition. Your love for me empowered me forty-six years later earth time to write this memoir now. In the spiritual reality, there is no time. You are with me still....

"Some day, after we have mastered the winds, the waves, the tides, and gravity, we will harness for God the energies of love, and then for the second time in the history of the world, man will have discovered fire!"
— *Teilhard De Chardin*

"The greatest science in the world, in heaven and on earth, is love."
— *Mother Theresa*

"Even so large as the universe outside is the universe within the lotus of the heart. Within it are heaven and earth, the sun, the moon, the lightning and all the stars...."
— *Upanishads*

"There can be no transforming of darkness into light and of apathy into movement without emotion."
— *Carl Jung*

"We each have the ability encoded in our very own hearts to create our life anew, to heal our body, mind, and spirit. I find that very empowering for the fate of humanity."
— *Jasmina Agrillo Scherr*

"Guru, God, and Self are one."
— *Ramana Maharshi*

# Contents

# Introduction

$\mathcal{H}$ave you ever wondered, woken up in the dark of the night, longing for something you don't even know? Do you have moments where you feel your power, your greatness calling to you? Who you are in your life, the world, the universe? Your purpose?

Since I was a little girl, I have been fascinated by the characters in fairytales and myths. I was fascinated by how the hero, plagued with seemingly impossible situations, is aided by divine intervention in some way, and survives by sheer wit, courage, and intuition. All those fairytale and mythological characters are us: divinely human, groping our way in the dark with our soul light to show the way.

We are not alone. The universal forces through our fellow human travelers, our spirit guides in nature and the spiritual realms are drawn to help us. We are human mirrors of the divine, with all the forces of the universe inside our hearts at our beck and call. We are finding our way home to the divine human we really are.

We are all called. This is my story of how I answered the call. The universe answers the call to which I refer through adversity and failure, as well as through success. Through the challenges I have had to overcome, I know my life to be an odyssey, an adventure, in becoming who I am.

As you read through the vignettes of my life story, may you feel your greatness calling to you, revealing itself through your own life story. Perhaps a memory, a feeling, an image, or a sensation surfaces while you read a passage. I invite you to take a break when you feel the urge—to pause, breathe, reflect with a notebook handy and a pen (your ready sword of truth) poised to record your insights.

Every path we choose to walk on the spiritual journey is valid as it takes us to our greatness and oneness with our own unique connection to the universe. Join me as I encounter the souls, and the life situations that have mirrored for me the lessons and wisdom of who I really am and have yet to be. I invite you to delve deeper into the meaning and wisdom about your own life reflected in my story.

Enjoy the story. Happy trails.
Love,

*Jasmina*

# Prologue

*December 2009*

*I* am shopping at a dollar store outside of Melbourne, Australia, in the small mountain village of Kallista. My fiancé, the clerk, and myself are the only people in the old time store.... The discount shirt looks like a good buy for $10.00. I feel a slight electrical sensation on my skin. I turn to face a woman, a stranger standing a foot away. She looks at me and speaks as if she were expecting to meet with me. She seems to know everything about me. In a clear, firm voice, she says the name of the healer I was with in South America three weeks ago.

"I have a message for you! Spirit wants you to bring your message of healing to the world. Spirit will guide you and is waiting to speak through you." My sense of time and place collapses.

Part One

# Wheel of Karma

O cosmic birther of all radiance and vibration!
Soften the ground of our being and carve out a space within us
where your presence can abide.
Fill us with your creativity so that we may be empowered to
bear the fruit of our mission.
Let each of our actions bear fruit in
accordance with our desire.
Endow us with the wisdom to produce and
share what each being needs to grow and flourish.
Untie the tangled threads of destiny that bind us,
As we release others from the entanglements
of past mistakes.
Do not let us be seduced by that which would
divert us from our true purpose,
But Illuminate the opportunities of the
Present Moment.
For you are the ground and the fruitful vision,
The Birth Power and the Fulfillment,
And All is gathered and made whole once again

*— The Lord's Prayer translated from the ancient Aramaic into English*
*by Mark Hathaway*

Messina Earthquake Survivors December 1908,
Photo by Comerio Luca (1878-1940)

# 1. Great Grandmother

$I$ never knew about your short brave life until I was twenty-nine years old. The great earthquake on December 28, 1908 in Messina, Sicily swallowed your body, but not your spirit. Your son, my grandfather, told me about you before he died. Since then, your death has made deep roots in my heart. Those roots extend deep into the center of the earth that took your life. I have often wondered what you looked like, what you wore. I don't even know your name or how old you were when you died.

When they pulled the collapsed walls and roof from your crushed body, they found my two-year-old grandfather and his older sister, alive, in your broken arms. Your final act was an act of divine mother love. You held them close, one in each arm. Your broken arms saved their lives.

My great grandfather in his grief married your sister, Felicia, who became the mother of your children, and off they came to America. Your life story lives in my blood still.

# 2. Grandfather

$G$rampy Charlie, my paternal grandfather, earthquake survivor. You have been in the spiritual plane, the other side of ordinary reality, for decades. When I see you in my mind now, you are glowing with golden light—you still look like you did in my youth—your short stocky physique, baldhead, gold-rimmed spectacles, and your signature Sicilian nose that thank God I didn't inherit. Yet, you are here now holding my ten-year-old wish to publish a book—supporting me—to write it now. Be here now! You are holding my book in your hands. "See!" you say, "It is already written and published." Aah, Grampy Charlie, you have my love.... He chuckles with his dry sense of humor that nobody notices because it is so dry.

*February 1968. Evening time. In Grampy Charlie's kitchen.* "It's all in your mind," he told me that very first time so long ago. I am twelve years old, sick and tired of suffering with this bronchitis haunting me for over a month. I am not exactly looking forward to going to sleep with this coughing and wheezing. As a matter of fact, I can't get to sleep.

My grandfather and I are sitting around the kitchen table, the yellow walls brightening my depressed mood. Grampy was in his usual calm, enigmatic manner, Sicilian style—simple, direct, and with a lot of fire underneath. "See. I have this pill here. You take this pill and it'll all be gone in the morning."

"Really?!"

"Yeah. I'm telling you." The enigmatic smile.

I take it secure in the comfort of my grandfather's love for me. I go to sleep in the den wrapped in the arms of the white pill's healing powers.

I wake up the next morning and...Oh...oh.... Do you believe it? Oh, my God! It's gone. No bronchitis. Not a trace of it. A miracle! I ponder it as the day goes by, watching my favorite *Star Trek* show on TV, eating Grandmother Jenny's delicious Sicilian delicacies. Nighttime again. "Okay," I say to myself, "I gotta ask him."

"Grampy. I don't think there is a cure for bronchitis with a pill. I don't...well...is there? What was in that pill?"

His usual enigmatic dry chuckle. "It was aspirin. See?" he says. "I told you. It was all in your mind."

I never forgot that lesson. Grampy, I am talking to you now because I feel you in my heart. I have done my best my whole life to live that lesson. Little did I know at the age of twelve how much I would need it in healing myself at a later age when I was nearly dead from an undiagnosed brain tumor.

Jasmina 1958, Photo by Charles Nunzio Agrillo

# 3. New Beginning

*Boston, Mass. April 28, 1956. 2:03 PM.*

$E$very birth is a significant event. I have feelings more than memory. It starts with a confinement, contentment, at home in the watery world. Then comes a bursting from the waters of life. My soul still knows from where it came. This new reality is a little loud, with sensations and sights that somehow are a little scary. My family welcomes me.

Where I am now is different. Much coarser. I have less freedom of movement in the confinement of a body. I sense in my feeling self because I have not yet developed my ego identity. Yet, I know I have done this before many times. Even though I am an infant, I still have locked in my soul memories of having lived before and the lessons I agreed upon to learn in this new life—to love, to serve, to grow in the light of unconditional love. I know I will be tested in the fires of suffering to birth the heart of fire that heals.

My earliest conscious memory is my white and yellow high chair—and the sea of familiar faces of my parents, grandparents, and my Aunt. I am saying my first word—a Sicilian meatball in Sicilian dialect. They are happy at my accomplishment, yet I am afraid of so much attention on my shy soul.

When I was seven years old, I began to consciously experience the connection to the world of light and spirit. We children were put to bed very early in those days. Stay-at-home mothers needed a break at 6:30 PM. Sharing a bedroom with my five-year-old sister, Deb, I could hear her talking to herself. I wish she would just go to sleep. I am bored. Can't go to sleep. So I lay in my bed. Yes, I know! I will play a game for myself. No one will ever know—so my mother couldn't hear me. I lay very still...my eyes closed, breathing. I imagined what it would be like if I had never lived at all—ever.... I found myself suspended in this nothingness, this blackness...and a spinning like flying through the nothingness. It was scary. I couldn't fathom it.

And then, sometimes, with my mind, I could travel through space to wherever my parents were in the house. And I could hear every word they said. On some nights, while waiting for sleep to come, I often heard celestial singing and felt the protection of angelic presences around me. I would pray to them to help me and my family, especially my mother.

One day, I shared my night experiences with my mother and she, not understanding, wanted to take me to a doctor to examine my head. It was then that I began to fear my own connection—a split in my psyche from the richness of my inner experience with my outer reality. It has been the task of my life to heal that split in my brain, and in my heart.

After that, I prayed for the nighttime sojourns in spirit to stop. Yet, at times, they were spontaneous and a comfort. Although I couldn't stop them, they saved my psyche from the effects of the chaos of my outer life.

Intense emotional memories are forever etched in our minds, with the visual clarity of an HD video. I was in the second grade in parochial school, sitting at my desk, bored, watching the clock in the early afternoon.

Sister Antonia is strict. I don't like her. I am afraid of her. She hits the children sometimes. I try to be as invisible as possible so she won't notice me and find something to yell at me about. The best way to do that is to lower my eyes and look down at my desk.

The load speaker comes on. "President Kennedy has been shot. He is in critical condition in the hospital. Let us all join in prayer for our president, his family, and our country. Class will be dismissed early." I don't understand. *Our president shot? What does that mean?*

Sister Antonia's face looks stricken, confused. Waves of despair and grief wash over our classroom. The waves spread all the way to my house, everyone I see. Everywhere. All over the nation and the world. In the gloom, I wonder: *Is everywhere the same? How can this be? Why? Where is safety?*

The whole nation and the schools shut down in honor of our assassinated president. On the day of the funeral, I watched on our black and white screened TV, fascinated by the national expression of grief, our first lady, Jackie Kennedy, her grief-stricken, shocked face revealed through the delicate black veil, holding the hands of her two children, Caroline and John, surrounded by a sea of national mourners—the sounds of the final military salute ushering in a new age of disenchantment and uncertainty in our American soul.

*Winter 1964.* The chaos of my family life and the emotional virus of grief, paranoia, and fear that infected America fanned the flames of a fear of life already lying in wait for my seven-year-old self. Sister Antonia used to lecture us on the fires of hell—the suffering for sinners who do not repent. I never believed her because I always knew God was Love. Yet, at such a tender age, I had a hard time reconciling that with the fear and chaos I felt around me. The fear of life settled itself in the very gut of me.

It seemed to come out of nowhere without warning—the pain, the cramps. It hurt so bad I got up the courage to overcome my fear and shyness and confide to Sister Antonia through my tears the pain and nausea in my belly. My mother came to school and brought me home. In the wee morning hours, Uncle Enzo, the anesthesiologist, was woken from sleep, diagnosed acute appendicitis, braved a snowstorm, and met us at the hospital.

The abdominal pain took me over completely. I remember the pain as a burning yellow and red light that I surrendered to as I lay awake all night while lying in bed in my hospital gown. I know what hell is—it's physical, mental, emotional pain that seems like it will never go away. In the morning, my appendix was removed.

I spent a week at St. Elizabeth's Hospital in Boston. In those days, you weren't sent home right after a surgery. My seven-day stay in the children's ward at the hospital was a break from the stress of my home and school life and a rite of passage in illness, healing, and death. I loved playing with a little girl who had kidney disease. There was also the cute red-haired, freckled boy who liked to peek at us under the lavatory stall in the girls' restroom. He had cancer. Even as I played with them, I knew. I felt a sharp grip on my heart that told me they would not live long enough to grow up.

# 4. My Maternal Legacy

*I* grew up loving and fearing my mother at the same time. Living with her day-to-day manic episodes was like waiting for a bomb to explode. I never knew when it would go off or what would trigger it. As an adult, it has been my legacy to heal the mother in myself first by having compassion and understanding of the hurt I suffered, and then my mother's suffering, through the help of therapy, meditation, and by mothering my son.

My mother was born second generation of Italian immigrants from Avellino, a mountain village near Naples. Her relatives were true salt of the earth folks. My great grandfather survived the Great Depression by turning his front and backyard in Boston into a vegetable garden and keeping his money in his house instead of a bank. They were hardworking blue-collar practical folks with dreams of a better life in America. The hidden legacy within the lineage was alcoholism and depression.

My mother grew up in the lower income section of her town, feeling deprived of the opportunities that wealth could bring. She helped support her family by working at Woolworth's while attending high school; met my father at the store and was married at eighteen. By age twenty-three, she had three children. Under those conditions, how could she be expected to fully love another being she birthed into the world? My beautiful, dark-haired, green-eyed ivory-skinned aquiline-featured mother—deeply spiritual, artistic, brilliant intelligence, yet emotionally manic, sometimes violent, and often angry. You were my first great teacher.

I remember being eight years old, my brother and sister already in bed, myself sitting on the living room couch in the dark across from my mother. She was crying, pouring her confused, depressed thoughts out in run-on sentences. It was then I knew something was not okay with my mother. I wanted to help her but didn't know how. I wished my father who went to college in the evening or someone could help her.

And then there were the nights when my brother and sister and I were supposedly asleep in our beds. I could hear my mother with her repressed rage finding an outlet on my father. I could hear them wrestling on the floor—the thumping sounds of their bodies—my mother screaming like a wildcat while my father fended off the violence of my mother's fury. *What if one kills the other? Do I have to choose which one I would like to die? I love them both. Will I become an orphan? How will I live?* I snuggle down deep under the covers, quietly crying, so as not to wake my younger sister. I remember the Hansel and Gretel fairytale my mother would read to me in her saner moments. I am Gretel who defeated the evil witch and saved her brother. I will survive. I could feel the angelic presences around me comforting me to sleep.

I was the first-born daughter and the middle child. Many times in my life, my mother has referred to me as her spiritual child. Indeed, my soul came to absorb her suffering. I became her stand-in for her rage at God at the injustices of her life. The imprints of her emotionally manic episodes on my soul in the form of an ongoing verbal abuse that infrequently became physical abuse in childhood awakened an anger deep within my core that became a fierce lifelong passion for well-being and freedom. The legacy of physical and mental addictions of depression, feelings of unworthiness and anxiety, issues of trust and safety became my legacy to undo. I knew deep within my soul I came to not just heal myself but to bring healing to my entire family lineage.

# 5. Freedom Run

*T*he contrast of the suffering of emotional and physical cruelties with my secret inner life became the catalyst that launched me to leave the family nest. To seek refuge in the greater world where everyone eventually became my family. Growing up in the cultural mecca of Boston, I experienced not only my Italian roots but also the ethnic diversity of many races. I loved it and felt a kinship with the diversity around me. The wider world called to me.

We know deep inside our mission what we come to do in this life—our purpose. We know it around the age of ten to twelve years. I imagined myself as a missionary nun healing the sick in Africa, an author of mystical adventures, and an artist. At the age of ten, I knew I needed to leave home and that I would need money. Starting at age twelve I began saving money; first from babysitting earning 50 cents an hour, then jobs at age sixteen through high school at an Italian bakery and vegetable market to earn my freedom.

In 1974, when I graduated from high school, I had saved over $2100 dollars, which to me was a lot of money. Without my parents' blessing, I left home. Moved to Maine to earn a college degree in fine arts—which became the seed of my belief and acceptance of my creative life, along with hard won self sufficiency and trust in my own inner guidance against the odds.

# 6. Slide Zone

*A*s a teenager, I had the ability to go deep in a hypnosis trance. And so my friends liked to experiment on me to explore the possibilities of the hypnotic state. One time, being the good subject of hypnosis, I was hypnotized to the experience of a past life. I went somewhere to a place of emptiness and blackness. I became stuck there in an emotionally traumatic memory, and not able to come back to present reality. It took a while for my very frightened friends to bring me back.

During my early adult years, I came to know more about my past lives. It helped me to understand my motivations. I even explored one of those lives through research at the Boston Library, exploring and reading microfiche copies of early twentieth century London newspaper headlines. What I found correlated with my memories. Even so, I had to learn to let go of the obsessive memories to live my life in the present.

I had unwittingly entered a *slide zone,* the place outside time where the boundaries of past, present, and future realities unwind. I hadn't yet developed the ability to navigate my consciousness in those dimensions.

In a healing crisis laying in wait many years in the future, I learned it is not necessary to randomly go back in time to dig up past life memories. That can be very dangerous for the unprepared ego. If our soul allows an emotional memory to surface, then it is part of our spiritual journey that the soul lesson learned be acknowledged and the emotions healed. Our healing process does not require us to remember the details of having lived before.

# 7. A Mysterious Visitor at Dawn

My High School years passed by in a bewildering haze of disillusionment—with the Catholic Church; then Martin Luther King Jr. and Bobby Kennedys' assassinations, my best friend's nervous breakdown, and the alienation and loneliness in choosing to not follow my classmates deeper down the chaotic spiral of promiscuous sex and hardcore drugs. Has God abandoned us, left us to our insanity? I didn't want to believe that. But where was the alternative? The alternative was to withdraw into reading novels, working at my job and school, and hanging out with my small group of girlfriends. When the opportunity presented itself, alcohol offered consolation from the harsh reality of abandonment.

At the age of nineteen, as I awoke at dawn in my apartment in Portland, Maine, the light, as I opened my eyes, illuminated the solid presence of a spirit guide dressed in a dark gown and cloak, with beautiful lights flowing out of his eyes into mine. He spoke to me telepathically. His name was a long word in a language unknown to me, although I later came to understand the sound of the language to be similar to Sanskrit. He said that his name translated into English was Simon. He came to remind me that my life has purpose, meaning, and direction. He told me that I must start taking care of myself in all ways. He said he is always with me and that I can call on him whenever I need to. The image of his solid body started to fade with the dawn light. His visit gave me faith in the spiritual connection. I am known. I am being supported by invisible guides.

At that time in 1975, I was a student of fine art. My life was chaotic. I was often sick with allergies that stayed with every season. I was creating art, living hard under the influence of alcohol and marijuana. I was not sleeping well, not eating well,

21

and working until 4:00 AM at a Deli restaurant to pay the bills. The great sense of peace that was transmitted through the eyes of the mysterious being in my room at dawn stayed with me for days and years to come....

In those early adult years, the experience of meeting the mysterious guide in my room launched a seed of well being to inspire me to bring more balance to my hard living habits. I gradually began to change my life. I started eating and researching about healthy foods and energy healing. By the time I was twenty-nine years old, I had developed enough self-control over my hard-living habits to give up alcohol and marijuana. Three years after meeting Simon, I had received my first Transmission from Reiki master John Grey, and the confidence that, I, too, can become a conduit of healing light for myself and others.

# 8. Grampy Charlie's Basement

$\mathcal{F}$or some reason, a visit to Grampy Charlie's workshop in the basement was always a mysterious adventure. Occasionally on holidays from college, I would return to Massachusetts to stay with my parents and siblings. I didn't have a car back then, and talked my father into dropping me off at Grampy Charlie's. Visits with him were always like stepping out of time. He had an aura of peace and equanimity about him. My grandparents' apartment life was quiet, simple, and orderly, in sharp contrast to the chaos of my home life.

I was studying stone carving and needed to learn how to sharpen my carving tools on a lathe. On that day's visit, Grampy Charlie was to train me on the technique in his basement workshop. We had a delicious Italian style lunch lovingly prepared by my Nonna Jennie—lentil soup, chicken cutlets, Italian bread, and an olive oil/vinegar dressed salad.

And now it was time for the descent to the basement workshop. My grandfather moved slowly with deliberation and thought, to limp and drag his right leg that has been paralyzed from rheumatoid arthritis since he was in his mid-thirties. If it was painful, he never complained. I followed slowly behind him down the back two flights of stairs from the second floor apartment. I was awed to be invited into his special space. The wooden stairs to the basement creaked to announce our arrival at the sacred space.

He built it himself out of wood—the walls, the workbench, and the stools. The workspace smelled of old wood and basement dust. His tools were hung on the wall above the workbench. They looked well worn and decades old. A broken black rosary was hanging among the tools.

"Can I have that?"

"Of course. Let me fix it for you first." He looked surprised and chuckled. I have never heard my grandfather out and out laugh. My grandfather was the epitome of a Zen master in disguise, masquerading as the refrigerator installer repairman by day. Sicilian style, though. He could be very opinionated on certain topics. He had that old-fashioned old country attitude about women's place in the world. We enjoyed arguing that out.

"Thanks. Now I'll always have something to remind me of you." I put the rosary in my pocket. To this day, I still have that rosary.

With a twinkle in his eyes and the enigmatic smile like he knows the meaning to a joke that nobody else gets, he tells me — "I made you a sharpening lathe from a motor I had lying around. You can bring it back to Maine." I was totally surprised and impressed. I examined it. He made it out of a motor with an on/off switch, with a belt attached and metal tool rest while sharpening. He even made the tall bench for the lathe to sit on.

We spent the afternoon talking shop as we sharpened the tools I brought. We said goodbye as we loaded the lathe, the chair, and the bench in my father's car, along with the unseen presence of Grampy Charlie's unconditional love and support.

# 9. Footprints

*I*n 1978, I graduated with a B.F.A. from Maine College Of Art, not prepared to find a job in my field of sculpture, yet open to what I could do to earn a living by creating my job. Trusting in the connection to my intuition, I said, "Okay." The telephone book in my lap (This was before the Internet days, mind you.), I decided wherever the page opens I will call the number and create a job. I opened to a Crown and Bridge company. Thought, *Hey, I can sculpt. Maybe they need me to make teeth.* I called the number. The owner said, "We happen to be looking for someone right now."

I went in for an interview and ended up working from an entry level position to the top of the company within five years. That job became the bread and butter to support my explorations in energy healing and spiritual growth and supplied the money for my sculpture materials.

Soon after I graduated in 1978, I met, John, who was to be my husband for the next twenty-eight and a half years of my life. I felt a magnetic primal attraction to him right away. He was handsome, intelligent, with a machismo exterior that disguised a nature that was sensitive, wild and poetic. He was a master carpenter by trade.

We often know our destiny in a flash! So it was with me.... Soon after meeting him at the Civics Sandwhich shop in Portland, Maine, I one day found myself in a casual conversation with him. While casually talking to him, I briefly blanked out; time traveled in my consciousness and saw myself with him ten years down the road.

Many people have had similar experiences, where the wind of our destiny takes us to where we are going—to those we come to be with who are a blessing for us in our soul's evolution.

At the age of twenty-five, I felt mature and ready to take the step of marriage. I became a stepmom to John's daughter, who we helped raise together. I liked having a readymade family. I was used to nurturing and caring for the emotional needs of others. Being creative, having a greater spiritual calling to truly know from my own experience the divine connection of my soul was a challenge in family life — to be true to that calling *and* to be active in fulfilling my family responsibilities.

# 10. Echoes

$I$n my late twenties, my job as a dental lab technician, sculpting, and caring for my stepdaughter filled my life. Step parenting was much more of a challenge than I had expected. Yet, the bond of love grew over time. My bonus daughter was a true fairy child of the Maine woods—wild and free. She taught me much to parent as a friend, a sister, and aunt. Yet, the secret desire to have a child of my own lay dormant. It was a desire I dared not consciously choose to act upon. If I were to ever get pregnant, it would have to be by divine decree. Tempting the divine can be an interesting proposition.

The years went by—married life, making and exhibiting art. Yet, I felt there was so much more. My soul wanted to expand in consciousness. I started having dreams, images of snakes in myriads of colors, forms, and lights. I felt the energy within my body and soul as a fiery passion for a life beyond what I lived. I craved secretly for a brilliant timeless expansion. In contrast to my outward life, this inward fire possessed me.

I started spending hours in my studio—making a collage of a serpent king whose coiled body held the skeletal forms of geometric patterns and shapes moving and connecting. Plants began to speak to me. Nature began to reveal herself to me. My sculpting benefited from my opening to the secrets of nature. Our evolution of the plants from the sea became a theme for many years in my work—plants, babies and snakes—psyche and symbol.

I became drawn to Native American and Celtic spirituality. I began to go out in nature to experience my oneness in the Maine forest. My Celtic spiritual teacher taught me through sacred dance eurhythmy to enter with my consciousness and body the elements, for example: earth, water, fire, wind, and air. My affinity to the element of wind inspired me.

One day deep in the Maine woods, I stepped into a clearing — pine and birch trees all around me. I started to move. As the wind blew around me, rustling the leaves, I talked in my heart to the wind. I asked, "Will you move with me?" With my arms, my legs, my whole body, I moved and directed the wind. IT BEGAN TO MOVE WITH ME, IN WHATEVER DIRECTION I MOVED! THE TREES MIRRORED WITH THEIR BOUGHS OF LEAVES MY PATH WITH THE WIND.

*I am fifty-seven years old as I write this memoir. Memory is like the yo-yos we used to play with as kids. You cast the desire to remember out and a memory unravels. Sometimes, it gets stuck on the way back to conscious retrieval. You rewind and cast again and memory unravels in fits and starts — sometimes smooth rolling, sometimes not. My early life memories are unraveling still.... Those years in my twenties began my apprenticeship to opening to the energy abounding in nature.*

I have found the secret of oneness is in letting go of the ego self with its thoughts and emotions, and then genuinely opening *to the universal presence in all forms of life.* Rocks, trees, animals, the elements, our fellow humans open when you talk to them with your gratitude and curiosity. The crows can warn you, the wind can whisper inspiration, the water can cleanse you, and the fire can give you energy. I often go out in nature to find the solutions to my most vexing problems and to restore peace, balance, and healing.

One such experience in my explorations of nature was to enter into the solidity of rockness. One day in my late twenties, I went to the rocky coastline of Crescent Beach, in Cape Elizabeth.

Climbing over rocks with the goal to find the special rock that spoke to me, I wanted to know what it is like to be trapped in matter — solid, immobile, and hard.

I sat in stillness. I addressed the rock, "Will you let me go inside you?" I felt a yes! I found my awareness deep inside the solid grey matter of rockness. Felt its immobility. Its solid strength. Inside the rock I experienced a rock memory. A little girl with her Dad. She was wearing a red raincoat, sneakers, and long blond hair as she stepped on my spirit body inside the rock.

A few weeks later while driving home from one of my beach excursions, I saw the little girl with the red raincoat holding the hand of her father while walking up High St. in Portland. Ah — synchronicity affirming my experience.

Sound energies abound in nature. In my many experiences with sound, the blessed coast of Maine with all its pristine primeval energies became my studio. My friend Barb at the beach said, "Do you know that you can chant OM to the periwinkles? Do you want to see what happens?"

"Let's do it," I said. I held a periwinkle up close. We chanted, Ommmm.... The periwinkle in my hand lifted its entire soft body out of its shell, waving its tentacles to the OM sound. When I stopped chanting it went back into its shell. We repeated this a few more times with the same result.

# 11. January 1989: A Cold Winter Night in Maine, a Wish.

*I* am sitting in my favorite tattered gold heirloom comfort chair. A bitter cold wind rattles the windowpanes. Someday, we will replace the window. For now, caulking will have to keep the cold out.

The book, *Autobiography of a Yogi*, is open on my lap. I dream often of returning to India. I was there last fall. As I read of the extraordinary yogis Swami Yogananda met while taking his disciples on spiritual pilgrimage — I am looking at his center, the Self-Realization Fellowship in the Pacific Palisades, Ca, with the windmill house by the lake. How exotic. I would love to go there someday. But I can't imagine that ever happening. It's on the other side of the continent. Nice thought though.

# 12. Grampy Charlie's Kitchen, 1991

Nonna Jenny and I are sitting at the 1950's style kitchen table, the late afternoon sun casting a soft golden light into the room — making the washing machine, the hardware of the sink, cabinets, and the metal face of the toaster sparkle. "Nana, I visited Grampy in a dream last night."

Grampy Charlie passed into Spirit in the fall of 1987 at the age of eighty-one. The last time I saw him was at the nursing home. He had the same equilibrium as always, even as he knew in the quiet space of his heart that he was next of his relatives to die.

We sat in silence on that visit in the nursing home. He had the familiar look in the aura around him, and in his skin, of someone soon to cross over. I knew in my heart, too, that it might be the last time I would be in his physical presence. I stood in back of him sitting in the chair — kissed the crown of his head and said, "Goodbye." He didn't say goodbye back. Just silence.

It has been one of the blessings of my life to be able to connect to the multidimensional aspect of being. During meditation and lucid dreaming, I have met in the astral world deceased loved ones as well as folks I would later meet and those who I did not know in this life.

In this astral dream, I found myself with Grampy Charlie. He was radiant in golden light illuminating his body and eyes. The rheumatoid paralyzed right leg condition was gone. He still looked like my grandfather, only lighter and younger.

"What are you doing here? You're not supposed to be here."

"I came because I am missing you and want to see how you are doing."

Grampy Charlie was a very *practical* Zen master in disguise, not necessarily eager to share his wisdom, never one to waste words, and always very direct. We were sitting in Grampy Charlie's yellow walled kitchen. Nana Jenny and Aunt Jo were moving about getting their breakfast ready. He was sitting at his customary place at the table close to the window so that he could see everything coming and going from the dining room and den.

He was looking at me with a twinkle in his eyes as he laughed at pulling a fast one on my grandmother and aunt. "I have been here all along—I'm with them all the time—only they don't know it. I sleep next to Jenny every night. I sit at the table and eat with them every meal, only they don't know I'm here."

I could see he totally enjoyed getting the last joke on them as he watched them move about the kitchen. "Okay it's time for you to go back now," he reminded me. I told him I loved him. Gave a hug and woke up satisfied we are still connected.

I told the dream to Nana Jenny. She was deeply touched and matter of factly said, "Well. That's why I always leave a space for him in bed and at the kitchen table."

Nineteen years later, Nana Jenny passed on at ninety-six years of age. We shared a connection to the spiritual realms of angels. I visited her when I was in the Boston area to see my clients in Brookline. In the den room next to the kitchen, we prayed on our beads together.

"I see angels, you know. I don't like to talk about it much though. 'Cause people don't believe me."

"I believe you, Nana. I see them too. Mostly, I hear them."

"I always knew it was you, the 'quiet one'. No one thought it was you. But I always knew. You were the smart one—you got away from the family." It felt good to have that acknowledgment.

"I'm ready for God to call me home. I've been ready for a while now."

I wanted God to call her home, too. At ninety-four, her body looked like an old tree with lots of bark, bumps, and age spots. She had a stroke recently that left one side of her face and eye paralyzed.

The last two years of her life she was in and out of the emergency room. The last time she was at home when the final stroke came. When my aunt wanted to call emergency, she said, "No—let me go." I know Grampy Charlie came to escort her into the light.

# 13. Secret Desires

*Y*ou know beloveds, that we sometimes get wind of a premonition that a secret desire is about to be fulfilled. Secret desires are stealthy. We barely can admit them to ourselves consciously. They have a way of flashing themselves up from our deepest subconscious. We barely recognize for fear to admit them. Yet, they build their desire energy underground and emerge as a manifestation taking us by surprise — ooops, where did that come from?

At age thirty, a long hidden desire came to fruition. I met one of the significant persons to influence my life and heal the mother wounds of my childhood, and give me confidence in my feminine nature — To love, to nurture the worth of my soul, and the belongingness to open more fully to the world around me. Shri AnandiMa is one of the living spiritual masters on our planet. She is an emanation of the Divine Feminine who can awaken that in others.

I met her at a public meditation program in Portland Maine in 1986. In my meditation, I went deep into the core of my being and saw the red coil of energy that had been haunting my paintings and drawings come alive and rise up in my body like a fire.

Being in AnandiMa's presence awakened the memory of a long hidden desire — I was twelve years old in a Catholic school. We often read from the New Testament the stories of Jesus and the disciples. I thought, *I wish I could experience what it's like to be a disciple to Christ. Why do I have to read about something that happened so long ago? I want to experience what it is like to be a disciple to Christ now.*

After that memory resurfaced from the first meditation in AnandiMa's presence, I knew it was my destiny, the deep desire so long ago being fulfilled, to enter into the guru-disciple relationship. I took formal initiation into the Kundalini Maha lineage through AnandiMa. In my many years of close discipleship, she became like a mother, soul sister, and friend — restoring my faith in my own connection to the Divine Feminine to the extent I became a mother to my son Ian, at the age of thirty-nine.

By the time I met AnandiMa, I was willing and ready to take responsibility for my spiritual growth through a regular practice. My spiritual apprenticeship to the path of Kundalini meditation, which is a path of raja yoga, unfolded over a period of fifteen years, over several trips of spiritual pilgrimage to India. Raja yoga is defined as the royal path of union, the path of meditation. The techniques of raja yoga can bring health to the body, peace to the emotions, and concentration of the mental forces to experience unity with our divine nature, our cosmic connection to the subtle forces of the universe.

What happens when we consciously take up the path, the responsibility for our spiritual evolution? Taking on the responsibility for our own spiritual growth comes through consistent every day awareness and practice. We are in the age of the magic pill — a pill for everything. The pill comes with a great cost and side effects. They can't give us the experience of oneness with soul, nature and the universe.

You reach a point when you know there is more to this physical reality, our relationships, our jobs, our habits. We long for something. We don't know what it is. We know there is something more. Everything dies eventually. We suffer. Even happiness in the outer things does not last. Nothing in our earthly life lasts. At age thirty, I had this realization.

*Bronze statue by Jasmina*

All those who came to me for Shaktipat are worthy,
And all of them are my spiritual heirs.
For my energy works through them.

*— Sri Dhyanyogi Madasudandas,*
*1878 - August 29, 1994*

# 14. Earth Angel

*W*hen the student is ready, the teacher comes. After receiving spiritual initiation, Sri Dhyanyogi, AnandiMa's spiritual master, began appearing in my dreams — like an Earth angel, guiding me a like a grandfather — taking walks with me in my dreams, where we would chat about daily things and he would advise me as a wise grandfather.

In one of many dream experiences of Dhyanyogi, I had returned to Maine from my first spiritual pilgrimage to India. My marriage was beginning to show signs of a gap between my spiritual expansion and my husband not inclined with that path. I was stressed. Culture shock really, between the heart opening experiences of India and the harshness and alienation that American life can be. My jaw actually locked from the emotional stress of returning to my life in America in 1988.

Substance abuse was an underlying issue in our marriage. When I became aware of John's addiction to alcohol and marijuana, I also became aware of my own. Besides being very allergic to alcohol, I liked how alcohol brought me out of my shyness and marijuana put my mind to sleep. In secret from John, I attended Al-Anon family group meetings in the hopes of understanding his addiction and gaining control of my own. By the time I had come back from my first spiritual pilgrimage in India at age thirty-two, I had been sober for three years. In my stress of coping with my marriage and life in America — I was considering returning to alcohol again to ease the emotional pain.

Guruji came to me in a dream. We were riding in the backseat of a car. He said to me, "Whatever you do — do not return to drinking. It is very negative to spiritual growth."

I answered back like the granddaughter disciple I was and said, "I was just thinking about it. I haven't done it yet."

"Well", he says. Whatever you do, don't do it." I felt chastised in a loving way and strengthened to not go back to alcohol. To this day, I have kept that promise.

In another dream in that period, he came to free me. Worry is a very negative emotion, a big obstacle in the spiritual path that has a very negative effect on our physiology, which I later experienced in my healing crisis years later.

I often worried about my mother. And have tried several times to get professional help for her to cope with her emotional mania and depression. To no avail. She wasn't ready for help. It was the kind of worry that was in the background, draining my energy.

In the dream, Guruji, again in the car, came to relieve me. He said, "Worrying about your mother is holding you back in your spiritual evolution. Give her to me. God and I are taking care of her."

# 15. God Saves My Life

*A*s a sculptor, I enjoyed volunteering my time in service to the disciple community. In the summer of 1990, I took on the project of directing the design and construction of fire pits in sacred geometric shapes for our mantra offering into the flames. Vedic fire ceremonies or *yagnas* are done to cleanse negative energies, and receive blessings of all kinds. They involve ritual offerings such as ghee, rice, and sacred herbs, along with the recitations of mantras.

On this occasion, I was driving on the freeway in Rhode Island to the fire ceremony project in my old Dodge K-Car. Happily driving along at a steady 70 miles per hour in rush hour traffic with all lanes filled, I noticed my car was overheating fast — all of a sudden, the engine starts sputtering out. *Oh, my God. This could be my death — and other deaths as well.* Then I prayed hard and fast, my heart rapidly beating that I thought I was having a heart attack. I prayed to my Guru, "I am in trouble. Help...help me."

Dhyanyogi gave all his disciples a blessing upon initiation into his lineage. Whenever we are in any trouble we may call upon God's help through a *sankalpa*, which is a Sanskrit word meaning "divine command." To empower the energy of the *sankalpa*, we are to say it three times. I said it, letting all the fear become the most passionate plea I have ever done in my life.

The engine started making a loud knocking sound, shaking the car and sputtering back to life. It went on for a few miles and again started sputtering out — I kept praying the *sankalpa* and the engine sputtered back to life. This kept happening for about fifteen miles until I could get off the next exit to a gas station. You know what they found when the attendant opened the hood?

"How long were you driving with the engine like this?"

"Oh, about fifteen miles," I said.

"Your timing belt is broken, along with other goings on in your engine. A car cannot run without a timing belt. The engine will immediately stop."

I was stunned. I just experienced an extraordinary miracle. As the story goes with my old car, it took a week to get all the parts to rebuild the engine. When it came time to have my car towed back to Maine, they were still talking about the miracle. My service project designing the fire pits went well, and we had a glorious Vedic fire ceremony. It even rained, which is an auspicious omen. Not a cloud in the sky on that hot summer day, until the clouds gathered over our offerings into the fire and the rains came.

# 16. I Visit the Spiritual Realms and Ask an Important Question

*E*ven now, decades later, the event remains as vividly real and miraculous as on the morning it happened ... *December 11, 1990, 5 A.M.* I lay awake with my eyes closed in my bed when I felt an acceleration of energy in my body and a flying sensation. Then I found myself walking through many rooms (more like enclosures), whose walls would dissolve and reappear, like a kaleidoscope of images, only I was at the same time moving through them.

I understood and saw that there were beings in those rooms living at various states of consciousness; however, a sense of purpose and detachment kept me from lingering in any of them. When I got through the rooms, I came out into a vast twilight space that was filled with countless numbers of beings. It was really like an ocean of souls!

At this time, I became aware of the reality of my situation — that I was lying on my bed, connected to my body by a psychic thread, and that I had a limited time where I was before I had to go back into my body. As I looked around me, I saw there were souls who looked like real flesh and blood people and then others whose form was transparent.

Some of these beings were looking expectantly off into the distance as if they were waiting for something to happen. Then, on the horizon, and moving quickly among the waves of souls, I saw a form that radiated tremendous rays of golden light. As the form came closer, I knew without a doubt this was Christ. I thought, *OH MY GOD!! THIS IS CHRIST!! I can't believe I am really here! This is really happening to me!* It became apparent we were all there to receive *darshan*. I was so struck with awe I couldn't move—only stare at the beautiful *Divine/Human* form approaching me.

Some of those He passed among He lovingly gazed upon or touched. Still others passed Him by as if they didn't see Him; and those waiting were reaching to touch his garments or bowing as He passed. Such looks of love and devotion that passed between recipient and receiver! As He came closer, every cell and hair of my body stood at attention. Then He came and stood very close to me, and I looked long and deep at His beautiful Form so as to remember everything—the eyes that were large and blue yet could be a deep dark brown, His olive skin and long, wavy, light brown hair—the garments he wore—a red robe and an inner white gown.

Incredible waves of compassion and love radiated from His eyes into mine. Then I bowed before Him, my head at His feet. Some time passed this way...waves of bliss emanating from the feet as if all wisdom, knowledge of the universe were contained there. Overcome with feelings of love and devotion, I lifted the white muslin robe that covered His feet (all my five senses were intact—I could feel the texture of the cloth) and kissed them....

My six o'clock alarm went off, which normally awakens me for a shower and spiritual practices. Some desire remained in my mind to see the Lord as Christ once again—so I turned the alarm off, lay back down, and drifted into a peaceful, dark state of mind like sleep...and found myself in a room that had the same twilight glow as if the light source came from within itself and not from any direct source.

In the room was a woman with very long, dark wavy hair who emanated strong vibrations of peace; while outside, Christ was walking about giving blessings (as before) to the countless numbers of souls waiting there. Although I also wanted to be outside for *darshan,* I felt moved to stay with the woman who in essence was very like Mary.

Then He came into the room and placed in my hands a white bowl of warm liquid ghee that had the most wonderful aroma and said, *"You may if you like"* — and in my mind I knew He was inviting me to massage His feet. I was thrilled beyond words that it was even possible for someone like myself to have such an honor.

He sat in a chair and very patiently waited for me to begin. I dipped my hands in the ghee and He gave me His right foot, which I slowly, deeply massaged. It was an incredible experience because His feet radiated such a vibration of love. Being in His presence felt very comfortable on a personal level and I asked, "Are you really Omnipresent? How can that be?"

He replied, "Yes, it can be done. I can be everywhere at once, can hear the calls and come to the aid of many souls on earth as well as the other planes. I always work this way."

I finished massaging His right foot and got up to get a silk cloth to use as a towel. When I returned, He was gone. The bowl of ghee was still there, as was the rug on which He laid His feet. The woman in the room (Was she the Mary of Jesus' mother or His beloved Mary Magdalene?) said, "Don't worry. He said He would be back."

I opened my eyes and found myself awake on my bed, an hour gone by. The bliss from the *darshan* remained for a long time. For several days afterward, *this* reality seemed very strange and unreal in comparison to the experience I was blessed to receive. It's one thing to want Grace; another to have it and know it's always there.

# 17. Flower Spirits

*I am seeing a giant white rose with petals like a lotus; in the center is a dark vortex with light inside taking me into the book I am downloading to you from the universe of my soul. I enter in and flying through where I left off on the spiritual growth, healing miracles, of my life that is inspiring folks all over the world to take up the spiritual journey to the center of their divine self and live it in this life....*

Flowers are special guides, a bridge between the spiritual world and the physical. In my life, I often left a fresh cut flower that would live for several weeks in water with no signs of decay — the water fresh. Or the flower will live for several weeks out of water — a single flower placed on my altar.

Flowers, dear beloveds, are your healing spirits. They gladly are here to assist in healing any trauma to your body, mind, and spirit. You only need to be in their presence, to breathe your flower in and ask that its healing fragrance and energy enter into you.

One of my brain tumor surgery recovery strategies during the winter in Maine was to sit or stand with my walker in a greenhouse to breathe in the green and the flowers of the plants. I had flowers in my room at all times to heal and remind me how much I wanted to live to become completely well. An amaryllis once bloomed three times during the spring season, which is rare.

# 18. The Crow Saves Ian

*Late winter in Maine, 1998. Our family walk on Mackworth Island.* We so look forward to our family walk around the island. Mackworth Island is well known for its school for the deaf and the famous movie, *Children of a Lesser God*, starring William Hurt and Marlee Matlin.

For our family, it's known as Fairy Island. My son, Ian, and I had many adventures making fairy dwellings in the woods — structures of acorns, leaves, twigs and stone furniture and plates for our invisible fairy friends to live in and eat.

Today, it's cold. Snow's beginning to melt. Lots of icy patches over the trails, with clearing in some spots where the ground peeks through. Early March is an exciting time, with hints of the coming spring, which makes us impatient to get out in celebration. Our body and blood made ready for the uprising, for the new life pushing up under the ground. Ian at three years was feeling especially energetic, wild, and free — ready for an invigorating hike.

We decide to take the ocean trail around the island. Speckles of sunlight filtering through the pine trees light our way over icy patches of rock and dirt on the trail. Ian, partially walking, running, skipping over the icy patches leads the way; next, my husband, then I lagging behind on the trail. I become filled with the beauty, the fresh ocean air and the peace and invigoration of the nature connection. I look up. A crow seems to be following me over the treetops. I walk along...my Native American spiritual training kicks in....hmm maybe the crow is trying to tell me something. While walking, I send my mental intention WHAT ARE YOU TRYING TO TELL ME? up to the crow. A picture forms in my mind: I see Ian run out to the concrete dock on the shore — he slips on a large area of ice and was about to go over the edge into the ocean. *My God. Is there a concrete dock on the shore of this trail? I have taken this trail many times before, but I don't remember seeing it there.* I felt a mother's intuitive worry about my son's safety. I walked on — partially wondering maybe the crow's message is not what I think.

We walked on another twenty minutes...up ahead, I see the concrete dock. Ian starts to run towards the dock. I see the icy patch the crow showed to me and I stop Ian in time. THANK YOU, CROW.

# 19. Ian

*I* am a mother because of you at age thirty-nine. You are the great joy of my life, and I am so glad you were born. I always said if I got pregnant it would be an act of God. I secretly wanted a child, yet the conflict between all the unhealed trauma of my childhood and my passion for the creative life kept me from consciously letting it happen. And Papa and your half-sister Shasha kept me busy. Papa at age forty-five didn't know if he could start over again raising a family.

An act of God it was. No sooner than Papa and I laid eyes on you, we fell in love for life. You taught us how to love unconditionally under all kinds of challenges. More than that, my love for you and your love for me healed my childhood. It could have been no other way — you, beloved son, were the key.

When I found out I was pregnant with you, I had just returned from India three weeks prior. Papa and I conceived you in a high state of joy at being together again after a long separation while I was on spiritual pilgrimage in India.

I was concerned about your fetal health because I had still been taking malaria medication not knowing I had conceived you. There was a possible risk of birth defects with that medication. AnandiMa gave me a mantra to protect you as you grew in my womb. Every day, I made sure I said the mantra one hundred and eight times.

During my second trimester, I decided to stop saying the mantra, feeling that all was well with you in my uterus. On a retreat with AnandiMa and Dileepji, they asked if I was still saying the mantra. I confessed I wasn't. They have the gift of second sight. They said, "You are going to need it just as much at the end as you did at the beginning."

One time, when I was three months pregnant with you, I woke up at 3:00 AM. I saw your soul—a small blue orb of light hovering over my navel. You were attached by an energy cord that oscillated above my navel. I knew you were waiting to move into my womb home when the time was right.

Oh, and Ian...you spoke to me often once you were in my womb. Whenever you did, I always replied to you silently in my heart. When I went into labor at 8:00 AM on August 13, 1995, I asked you, "When do you intend to be born?" And I heard you say in my heart, "I want to be born at midnight."

*7:30 PM at Mercy Hospital, Portland, Maine.* The nurse examines me. "You are only three centimeters dilated. It looks like this baby will be born around 8:00 AM in the morning." *Sorry*, I said to you patiently waiting to be born, *you won't be born at midnight.*

*9:30 PM.* The nurse had just put me on the fetal monitor. "This is not good. The heart rate is not good. He's not getting enough oxygen." My extreme worry for your life became a passionate prayer to God and Guru, "Whatever it takes, spare his life. I want him out of my body."

We become heroes by default—not because we have to but because there is no other choice. I did everything I could for the next two and half hours to stay in a deep meditative awareness, labor pains included, to stay calm in my body and mind, while the midwife held her hand inside my vagina to prevent your head from moving deeper into the birth canal with every contraction. You see, you somehow managed to get tangled up in your umbilical cord.

You were born at 12:03 AM by emergency C-Section. My doctor later told me, "I have birthed hundreds of babies. I have seen this happen before. You can't tell me that baby didn't know when he wanted to be born. That baby got tangled up in his umbilical cord to make sure he was born at that particular time. He arranged it." *Knowing you now as a grown young man — you are a powerful force to reckon with when you have your mind made up.*

Ian, with your crystal eyes that can see into and beyond appearances: As an infant, your very large grey/ green/ blue and gold reflective eyes would stare at the family, friends and strangers that came to admire your beauty, without blinking — until they had to look away. Your brow would wrinkle as you continued to stare them down. "Why is he looking at me that way? Do I have three heads?" was a common response to your ceaseless peering.

When you were two and a half years old, you reminisced about a few past lives. Pointing at Guruji's picture on my altar, you very matter-of-factly said, "He's my friend from a long time ago. Only I was a very old man then."

"How old were you, Ian?"

Still pointing, you said, "As old as this house."

I calculated that to be around eighty-four years. "Were you in India with him then?"

"Yes."

On another occasion, we were talking about your paternal grandfather, Charlie, who was my Grampy Charlie's son, my dad. Your large crystal eyes intently gazing, you adamantly said, "He's my son."

"Ian, he is your grandfather."

"No!" you very adamantly said. "He is my son."

At four years of age, you were still in touch with your past life memories. We were having tea at a cafe in Berkeley. I had introduced you to Adam, a close friend I had traveled with in India. All the while Adam and I are getting caught up with travel memories, you were looking at Adam. Staring at him with that peering squinty stare.

"Do you know him from a long time ago?" I asked you.
"Yes. I do."

Ian, even though you are a grown young man and your face has grown to accommodate your very large crystal eyes, you still have the uncanny ability to see into the soul of people and the truth in life situations. May that gift always serve you well as you venture into the adult world to fulfill your soul's mission.

# Mantra to Remove Obstacles

*Om gam ganapataye namaha!*

*Loosely translated*: "Cosmic Sound! Wake up, Root Chakra, energy of transformation, Lord Ganesh of wisdom and peace, so I can move through any obstacles in my life. I honor you!"

# 20. *Samskaras* (Mind Impressions)

*I*n my spiritual training, I practiced mantras designed to burn the negative seeds of past experiences. As we are multidimensional beings — timeless — we have lived and are living in the past, present, and future simultaneously. The negative seeds (the imprints) of past thoughts and actions affect at the unconscious level the choices we make in our lives. Occasionally, the effects of those seeds come through as emotional waves of trauma seemingly out of nowhere acting and disrupting our consciousness and functioning in daily life.

While AnandiMa was visiting in Maine, I had a dream in which I met a Swami who I had never met before in my daily life. He was a living person with an ashram in Pennsylvania. We dream multidimensionally. We meet on the astral plane with friends, family and strangers, but mostly do not recall upon waking, except with a vague notion of having been with them. This swami in the dream told me to say a mantra to heal a *samskara* from my past. I did not know what needed to be healed.

AnandiMa interpreted my dream and gave me a Ganesh mantra to remove the obstacle that was blocking my spiritual growth. My homework was to do one mala a day of 108 repetitions for a number of months to clear this very significant mind impression.

So I sat in practice. Day after day. I stopped after two weeks. Depression and heaviness was slowing me down. I resisted the mala practice. I simply did not want to deal with the depressing heavy energy and decided to wait until I returned to India with AnandiMa to resume the practice.

## *India 1994. Bandhvad Ashram, Gurjarat. Out in the desert.*

I had decided to resume the Ganesh Mantra in the cave at the ashram, to allow the memory and the trauma to clear. Day after day for hours in the dark cave, in the heat of desert India, I said the mantra. How many times? Until I reached 120,000 recitations. As I finished the final 108 recitations I felt the first emotional waves surfacing from my deep unconscious. Despair. And then the thoughts came — unbidden, loud, and demanding — *Just go up to the top floor of the Ashram roof and jump! Do it! Do it now!*

By now, I felt the full force of the negative thought form. It unhinged me. I broke down. Then I relived the memory. I was in the body of an early American settler — a young woman in simple pioneer dress. I perched on a high bluff — and jumped backwards over the cliff — my arms outstretched like wings — my long, light brown hair flying out around me. Upon impact on the rocky ground, my spirit left my body and I went up into the sky! *I later researched the suicide phenomenon of early American women settlers. The numbers are approximately three thousand women took their lives, jumping down wells and over cliffs. Life was that harsh. Sometimes, we have no choice. Although in future life, we have to deal with the repercussions of the thought form tendency.*

How many times in this life have I contemplated taking my life in this way? Always the same way. When I get depressed at the intensity of my life, comes the impulse to jump off the bridge, into the river, or on to the highway, or from the building to the pavement. In the ashram cave, I broke down, my body shaking, my heart breaking open in waves of healing.... Later on, AnandiMa came by in my room at the Ashram. "You have a new life now. The past is gone. God and Guru took care of that for you."

This is what it can be like to take full responsibility for our own suffering and hence, our healing: To be patient. To bear our pain with love and care like a mother for a child. Grace comes, beloveds. It always comes when the heart cracks open. We have to ask for help. That is part of the surrender, the giving over for the grace to flow. Remember to always allow yourself to be humble enough to ask for Divine help. It always comes.

It is a challenge to embrace what is unacceptable, unforgiven in ourselves. Most of the spiritual journey is about that one thing—forgiveness—for ourselves and the others who are the mirror of that need. They play the roles of ourselves in the path to fullness in the light of divine living.

Through spiritual practice with the aid of mantra (sound vibration), I released and cleared the suicidal thought pattern that I had carried over for several lifetimes. One of the tasks we all are here to do on the planet at this time is to clear the traumas, wounds of the soul. We have the opportunity to do this at a tremendously accelerated pace.

Those of us on the planet who are not ready or attuned to this process will suffer more during this transition. If you are called to be reading this book now, you are on the other side of that and ready to take up your mission of clearing for the light to come through you. You may feel that you are unworthy, but no one is more worthy than you.

*Within your heart lies the connection to your divine worthiness. Remember a time when you felt your wholeness, your nobility, and your power. It can be in your childhood or anytime in your life. Re-experience the feelings in this moment. You have just reclaimed your empowerment. The world is waiting for your unique value and action to bring the light, the joy your gifts are to the world.*

There was a time in my early adult life when I thought I was too damaged by the chaos of my life experiences to live in joy and fulfillment. For some souls like myself, we chose to learn via the path of negativity. Through the contrast of not having what we desire, we learn what it is we *really* want in our life. We learn through pain and suffering; our expectations in relationships, education, money desires may go unfulfilled. The disappointments of failure tell us what we learned so that we can grow and have the desires that really matter in our life.

For instance, I didn't know what kind of beloved partner was best for me until I experienced the unhappiness in my first marriage. In a healing experience I had in South America, I spent an evening writing, filling both sides of a paper with all the qualities I would like my beloved new partner to have. I read it every day and then let it go to the universal manifestation bank to grow in appreciation. I helped feed the desire to grow by applying gratitude to this list daily. Gratitude is the frequency that will attract what you most desire in your life. And it's fun, too!

Sri AnandiMa and Jasmina at Shiva Temple,
Srinagar, Kashmir, 1988

# 21. Divine Service

Nowadays, there is so much guru demoting being done and rightfully understood in the context of corrupt spiritual leaders who are well represented in all spiritual traditions. The guru-disciple relationship is a mirror of the divine dance between our human self and the connection to the divine within ourselves. The guru is like a human stand-in for God until we can make the connection on our own. We get to act the story of the *lila* drama of enlightenment with another human being who is worthy of that role. So it was with Sri AnandiMa and Sri Dhyanyogi.

Not everyone needs a human guru. But I surely did. I honestly did not know how to love because I hadn't experienced it enough through my relationship with my mother and father. Our human parents are not perfect. Now that I am a parent, I feel the vulnerability of imperfection in the role of mother to my son.

I wanted to know what love is and I wanted to be shown before I could have the confidence to love myself and others. When I took spiritual initiation at the age of thirty, so began the conscious *lila* experience of unconditional love.

## Gujarat, India, 1991

Once while driving through the desert on our way to the Bhandvad Ashram, I had a desire to be held, to nap in AnandiMa's lap. We were sitting in the back of an old station wagon. AnandiMa heard in her mind my thought and offered me her lap to sleep in. I fell asleep in the deliciousness of naptime in the lap of the mother—just like a little baby, while she stroked my hair.

My spiritual evolvement came about because of that love—divine—yet through a human channel who lived in an awakened state of unconditional love. Over the years, in a close relationship with AnandiMa, the state of unconditional love became awakened in my own heart. I desired with my whole being to be worthy of the love through service in my artwork.

I was invited to cast Sri Dhyanyogi's feet and hands on my second trip to India in September of 1991. Words fail to describe the experience of bliss and fire in touching his feet and hands—a state of holy surrender while remaining fully conscious in the left brain task of casting with tools and materials. Through that experience of service, I no longer had the blind ambition I had as a young sculptor to be famous for my art—to be a big name in the New York art scene.

The step of devotion and service is an important part of being love. We have to know it and practice it sooner or later in whatever means we have available to us. The choice is ours.

# 22. *Samadhi* (Divine Communion)

$I$ was thirty years old when I met the Shaktipat master, Sri AnandiMa, who was to have the greatest influence on my life up until that time. In the fifteen years of my spiritual discipleship, I grew in my ability to enter deeper states of meditation, which took me into direct communion with the divine referred to in Sanskrit as *samadhi*.

Fire Ceremony in the spiritual traditions of India is a sacred offering to the fire for healing and spiritual evolution. Truly, witnessing and participating in the event has given me an experience of Heaven meeting Earth. When I look into my heart to recall past experience, my memory seems to be composed of two parts—the Outer Fire Ceremony and the Inner Fire Ceremony.

## *Yagna (Fire Ceremony) for World Peace, Rhode Island, 1994*

In the outer experience, I am helping to shape the fire *kunds* (altars) with bricks, mortar, cow dung, and clay. This is divine *seva* (service). The earth, materials we are using, and the sky elements, all know God is coming, and we work together, while the *shakti* flows through our hands to shape and form. It is hard physical work—we are tired, our backs ache, but we are exhilarated! And best of all is the sculpting of the seat of Brahma (God's Throne), the icing on the cake!

On the day of the fire ceremony, we are sitting around the *kunds*, the hot sun is blazing, wind is blowing smoke into our faces stinging our eyes, as we offer our mantra to the very large mouth of God—the fire pit. Our voices sound like bees buzzing around and around the beehive. We hope with all our hearts that God will hear our prayers.

Very often, a "sign" is made in the clouds forming over our ceremony and a little rain comes, making known the presence of God.

Then came the experience of the inner fire ceremony that completely altered my life forever. Sometimes, a major step towards self-realization requires a few steps backward to integrate the experience deeper into one's life. The memory of it is still vibrant, special, and sweet. On the day before the fire ceremony, while doing my spiritual practices to God, I asked, "Please give me the blessing of *samadhi* at the fire ceremony tomorrow." And then I forgot about it. On the day of the fire ceremony, I was very busy doing *seva*, and as the final offerings were being made, I remembered my *sankalpa* to God and thought, *Well, so much for that sankalpa. I've been too active to be in a meditative state.*

Then AnandiMa's assistant began reciting closing mantras to the Divine Mother, which became the sound of pure love to my ears, penetrating my sadness, disappointment, and longing. Waves of joy began to cause a pressure inside, releasing a flood of tears and heat. I felt an energy being directed at me externally and I turned my head to meet the gaze of Shri AnandiMa. Her eyes were large and full of bliss, and she was smiling at me.

Thoughts came into my head—her voice saying, *I'm going now. It's okay. You can come, too.* And then she *pranamed* and I *pranamed* back, then closed my eyes. A force of energy rose up within my body, like water breaking open a dam and then an explosion at the heart.

My physical body gave way and I fell back to the ground, landing gently, almost weightlessly. I could feel electric currents of energy flowing through and cleansing the *nadis*, pathways of energy, causing involuntary movements of my body. The experience reminds me of the sensation of sticking my fingers in an electric socket as a child; only here, the experience was much more subtle and prolonged.

My breath outwardly withdrew into the spiritual plane. At first, it felt like I was drowning, but then I got used to it, as if I were breathing under water. And then all bodily sensations ceased. During this first phase of the experience, I could hear disciples singing the hymn "*Om Jaya Jagadisha Hare*" — "Glory to the Lord of the Universe, whose every vibration is the pure joy of Creation." God must have been singing that hymn while creating the universe.

My consciousness became free, floating in what can only be described as an electric "ocean of love." I was aware of my soul as an individual wave in a great vibrational sea of love. And as an individual soul in God's ocean, I started asking questions of a deep nature, such as, "Who am I? Why am I here?" and receiving answers beyond words to those questions. Then, satisfied, I came to rest in the Ocean of Bliss for the entire time Shri AnandiMa was giving *darshan* over several hours. The Ocean of Bliss was also her *prana*, so I was experiencing that at the subtle level. I could even see occasionally the subtle body of disciples coming up for *darshan*, beautifully lit with a golden light.

I have no words to describe my experience of resting in the sea of Love, because there was no memory of experience. After a period of time, my *prana* started to withdraw from Her *prana*. I was intuitively told that Shri AnandiMa was ascending into the highest state of *samadhi*, and I was not ready to go there, so it was time for me to come out of meditation. Very slowly, my consciousness came back into my body, my breathing returned to normal, and I could hear sounds and feel cold air on my skin and the desire to move my body. For several hours after awakening, I felt weird in the sense of my consciousness, which is infinite, being stuffed into this physical body. During the entire experience, I was guided and protected by Shri AnandiMa's *prana*.

Over the years, I have learned that it is one thing to be given the grace to experience the presence of God, and another thing to become Love! And that has been a slow, ongoing process, enlightening and very often painful—letting go of what is not Love.

Ultimately, the purest form, highest form of fire ceremony takes place in ourselves. We surrender our whole being as we are in the present, like the sacrifice of a lover to the beloved, to become a sacred vehicle for divine energy to flow through. Eventually, the fire of divine presence burns away all the doubts, fears, and negativity in the storehouse of karma. Divine presence can then come to permanently reside in our hearts.

**Gaumukh, mouth of the Ganges, on Gangotri Glacier,
photo Courtesy of Yekaterina**

# 23. India Miracles

*I*ndia defies description. How can I describe the mystery of
India? It's everything. How can I describe the phenomenon?
Right away, India blasts you—its smells, from dung to roses
and sandalwood, saints and *sadhus* abound on every corner; as
does extreme poverty, dust, disease, beggars, and dying people
on the streets.

Growing up as an American, I wasn't used to seeing lepers
and beggars and people sleeping on the streets, and wondering
"Are they dead or alive?" Neither have I ever felt such life—
passionate, teeming life. And the energy, oh the spiritual energy
defies description. The land is saturated with electric spiritual

energy. With all that, you would think I would not want to be there. But I did. You know why?

Nothing is repressed. It's all there, right in front of your eyes—the full spectrum of the suffering and joy of being alive. In America, we know life is not a bowl of cherries. There is poverty, disease, and immense psychological suffering, but it is the kind of suffering behind closed doors. In India, it all hangs out together—the full spectrum, nothing hidden. Oh, yes, and the heat of India—external and internal—the dry 120 degree heat of the desert, the humidity that rises out of the ground and your body like steam, soaking your clothes as you stand still. India's internal heat is the land of kundalini fire as it blazes the spiritual fire of the pilgrim, burning away the debris of negative karma. What does heat do? It burns and clears. The element of fire burns the negativity from our bodies through fever and sickness and emotional disease from our mind and heart. Each of the many India pilgrimages of my life has been all about the external and internal fires.

## 1991, September

On this second trip after many years of intense spiritual practices, I was ready for a deeper level of soul cleansing than ever before. This spiritual pilgrimage was one of the truly major and most difficult endeavors of my life. We had originally planned on starting our Himalayan trek three weeks later. However, Guruji had us change our intineray at the last minute. He foresaw a natural disaster.

Our trip began with a few nights in Singapore on our way to Mumbai. It was there that I experienced inner *kundalini*, subtle energy sounds indicating the energy centers of my body were very stimulated. For the rest of the trip, I heard the *brahmanadi* sounds with the Om mantra while waking and sleeping. Someone would be casually talking to me while I was listening to internal loud booming sounds and the buzzing of bees. These are classic *kundalini* manifestations of the movement of the spiritual energy through the chakras along the spine. At other times, I would experience immense internal heat and high fevers. I often used milk with ghee or orange juice to control the internal heat.

On every pilgrimage we went on with Sri AnandiMa, Sri Dhyanyogi, through mastery in projecting his subtle body, would watch over us from his room in Ahmedabad, in Gujarat province. Our task on this trip was to take a treacherous journey to the mouth of the Ganges River at 14,638 feet deep in the glacier area of the Himalayas.

Our first overnight stop in Rishikesh in the foothills of the Himalayas began the official pilgrimage. Here is where we had a group ritual bathing for purification before beginning our *anusthan*. The whole trip to me now seems like it could have been a dream. We were in Rishikesh several days. During that time, I bathed in the Ganges at dawn and dusk, as well as group excursions to temples and the Shivananda Ashram. Luckily, we were allowed to meditate and have *darshan* in Yogi Shivananda's *samadhi* room. Sounds of mantras were bouncing off the walls and I wanted to stay and stay....

Our next stop was Uttarkashi. AnandiMa and the group went to a temple that her family priest was visiting and offering special mantras. I developed my first bout with sickness—a migraine followed by an intense fever and then sweating, so I didn't go. During the migraine, I started hearing the mantra *Hari Om Tat Sat* fairly loudly and continuously. I heard that mantra for the next seven days we were in the Himalayas. It is the official mantra of the formless presence of God in the Himalayas. Three weeks after our stay there, an earthquake that killed thousands of people demolished Uttarkashi.

Onward to Gangotri. At 10,000 feet elevation, most of us had some form of altitude sickness. The fever left me weak and then

73

I caught a cold and felt a little disappointed to not be in tip-top shape for the big trek, but I was still ecstatic to be there. Conditions were starting to get more primitive, and culture shock was beginning to set in among those of us who were there for the first time. By this time, I was hearing the sacred sound of OM in the land — the rocks, the sky inside and outside.

At Gangotri, our base camp, all roads end. We had a full day of trekking, a 14-kilometer climb to our overnight camp at 12,000 feet. We got up at dawn for an early morning start. That morning, I had the most delicious breakfast of my life — potato parathas cooked over coal, with fresh yogurt which I ate in deep silence outdoors, with the Om sound singing to me, a level of peace I have never experienced before.

I had my knapsack on and was ready to go when AnandiMa gave us *prasad* (blessed fruit) to begin our trek. *Aaah, mine was an apple — I feel like I'm home in Maine.* I got out my utility knife to cut a slice — oops, the knife slipped off the apple, slicing deep into my index finger — the blood spurting out. It wouldn't stop bleeding.

We had two doctors in our group, an oncologist and a veterinarian who gathered around to inspect my finger. They disagreed on the treatment. The oncologist thought it needed sutures; and the veterinarian, a butterfly bandage would do. We had neither of those supplies. Literally, this camp was in the middle of nowhere in the vastness of the Himalayas.

The oncologist, an Indian man, decided to take me up the trail in search of a cave clinic. I, in mild shock and pain and a little stoned from the Om sound, climbed an off the main trail path, with the oncologist holding my cloth-bandaged finger to control the bleeding, while a disciple followed behind carrying my knapsack...lo and behold...a *sadhu* in an orange robed sari and a huge walking stick happened by soon after we ascended the trail. They conferred in Hindi; *yes there was a cave*. We walked on....

We came up to a wooden door in the side of the mountain. We went in, to be transported in time back about one hundred years, by the looks of the single room in the cave. It was a primitive clinic, dirt floors, a wrought iron bed, and dirty mattress — lots of shelves with mysterious muddy liquids in glass jars on wooden shelves.

The doctor who did not look like a doctor — was unshaven with well lived in clothes, bloodshot eyes, and dirt under his fingernails — invited me to sit on a wooden crate while he examined my finger. My oncologist was the translator, "There are no sutures. He will do a butterfly bandage. There are no painkillers. But he has antibiotic medicine to prevent infection." We paid the makeshift doctor a small fee and descended back to our camp.

## The Trail

We left camp ascending the 14-kilometer trek to the overnight camp. It was cold. The kind of cold that seeps into your bones — you can never get warm enough. Sadhus passed me by with nothing on but a loincloth, a shawl, sandals or barefoot, and a walking stick.

I had a guide and a mule with my supplies. As I look back in memory — I was not in my normal left brain functioning. I was affected by the altitude, my finger throbbing; yet the saturated ground and sky vibrating Om soothed my shocked mind and pained body.

I sent my guide on ahead of me. I am not a horse or mule fan. To make matters worse, my mule liked to walk at the edge of the cliff face. Too scary for me with a healthy fear of heights. I saw someone being carried down the trail in a body bag. No thanks — goodbye, mule. I'll meet you on top. My guide went with the mule and my supplies.

How can I describe how breathtakingly beautiful and eternal are the Himalayan mountains? And how absolutely every rock, tree, soil, and the sky is permeated with the vibration of Om. On and on I walked. Someone saw me holding my bandaged finger up and made me a sling out of cloth. On and on I walked, the sun warming me up, every step slow and heavy. I couldn't walk at a brisk pace with my fast beating heart and labored breathing accommodating the high altitude. Sometimes, the trail in places was only a few feet wide, with the cliff dropping off hundreds of feet.

Hours go by. In my shocked condition, I dropped my water bottle. I don't remember when or where — didn't even feel it slip off my shoulder...a-a-h.... I left my snacks with my guide and the mule. On and on...I am thirsty...very thirsty and a little dizzy. I contemplated not making my camp by nightfall. Sleeping on the trail exposed to the elements and wild animals with the cliff beside me was not an option.

On and on...all I could think about was water. Please, I need water. No one on the trail for what seemed like hours. I was somewhere outside of time. I passed by J., who had an acute case of culture shock. He had a wild look in his eyes as he said, "I think I'm going to have a nervous breakdown. I can't take any more." I was thinking *you already are having a nervous breakdown, but you are going to be okay.* Instead, I said, "I know what you mean. I hear you."

On and on...I come upon my friend, K., collapsed, lying across the trail — an asthma attack, barely breathing. I completely forgot about my thirst. Her feet touched the edge of the five-foot trail dropping to hundreds of feet to the rocky basin below. K. had forgotten her asthma meds at the base camp.

I noticed two disciples were assisting her. Should I stay? I stayed for a while, holding a shawl over her with my one good arm to provide shade from the sun and chanting a mantra to offer healing support. How much longer should I stay? I would be lucky if I made it myself by nightfall. What if she died? I stepped over her.

On and on.... Here came Dan crashing down the trail at breakneck speed. "Water?" Water? Does someone need water? Guruji told me someone needs water," while waving the water bottle.

"Yes. It's me. I need water."

Dan told me Guruji has been talking to him in his head giving instructions to help those of us in trouble. Dan was young and physically fit. Guruji, mind you, was hundreds of miles away at that moment on the other side of India. My thirst quenched, Dan disappeared down the trail.

The next day, I found out Dan, under Guruji's instruction, came upon K., ran down the trail to the base camp to get her medicine, and ran back up. He felt he was given superhuman stamina under the circumstances. Her life was saved.

The last one quarter of the 14-kilometer trek to the camp, I walked with AnandiMa and Dileepji. They purposely left last on the trek to support those of us who were struggling behind. They caught up with me. I was not strong enough to keep up with the other disciples, and, towards the end, I just wanted to lie down on the trail and go to sleep.

Dileepji asked me, "Are you going to make it?" My love for them kept me going when my will was gone. So I kept walking, watching their feet, and their feet got me the rest of the way.

At twilight, I finally made it to the hostel camp, beyond pain, fear, hunger, and fatigue. There was no heat, electricity, or running water. I went into my room that I shared with ten other disciples and found most of them in bed, moaning how they couldn't bear to go on with the trek. Our supper seated around a wooden bench looked like something out of one of Van

Gogh's coal miner family paintings—kerosene light, coal smoke, human suffering and ecstasy combined. In the thick of the smoke, I ate chapattis, potatoes and dal, and shared a hostel bed with four other people. In the biting cold, I went to bed in full winter garments—boots and all—and snuggled in with the women. Even so, I still shivered all night.

The pilgrimage to the mouth of the Ganges in Gaumukh was an *anusthan* for the spiritual healing of myself, my husband, my parents, and the couple who sponsored my trip. An *anusthan* is a dedication of spiritual practices and or pilgrimage to relieve the suffering of oneself and others to advance spiritual evolution. Our goal was to gather the sacred water in copper vessels, one for each person named, at the source of the Ganges. Then to journey to Rameshwaran in the south of India and offer the sacred water in a special *puja* ritual performed in the Hindu temple. For those whose water was offered at Rameshwaran would definitely be liberated. However, that is according with the soul's desire as to whether it wants to take a body again, but the cycle is broken.

The next morning, surprisingly enough, we were all remarkably recovered, considering the circumstances. We trekked another 8 kilometers to the mouth of the Ganges at Gaumukh. As we drew closer to Gaumukh, I felt I had been carrying the weight of my *samskaras* (mind impressions) and it was being cleared through physical and emotional hardship and pain. I thought of those for whom I was offering the *anusthan*—John, my parents, and the couple who loaned me the money for the pilgrimage. Somehow, it made the hardship more bearable that I was walking for others as well as myself. I was shedding my old self with each step and becoming stronger and lighter as we came to the mouth of the Ganges at the region of the glaciers. Guruji's presence was very much with us, as we were completing the *anusthan* for him also.

78

The mouth is a large opening in the mountain from which the water gushes forth. We did purification rituals and received a baptismal blessing from AnandiMa. In the presence of the cold pristine air, the force of the water as it spurted over the large junks of glacial ice, with the glacial mountains as the backdrop, in awesome silence, we filled our copper vessels, holding on to each other as we leaned over the rocks. It has been predicted that in twenty years, this area will be enclosed by the encroaching glacier.

We didn't stay there for more than an hour. A low rumbling sound was heard throughout the mountains. At the advice of our tour guide, we left very quickly to avoid the possibility of an avalanche. Not very far from the mouth, we passed by on the return, a wall of rock and sand that came down on thirty-five pilgrims a month before. The bodies were still inside.

That same day, we had to descend the 26 kilometers back to our base camp at 10,000 feet. Words cannot describe the pain, fatigue, and fear that came with each one of us, and the spiritual strength, faith, and do or die resilience that blessed us to complete the pilgrimage.

As I descended the trail down from Gaumukh, I saw a very steep incline ahead of me. The trail was about two and a half feet wide and the rocks were sliding down the incline. I was too exhausted to walk—so it was the mule and my guide. With the Om sound blasting in my ears and a horrible fear as I couldn't help but look over the edge to the sharp boulders at the foot of the cliff, my mule and I ascended the incline. The Law of Attraction principles may not agree with my method, but the way I face my fears—I imagine in detail the worst scenario, then I keep looking at the scene long and hard to dissipate the fear. In this case, it was my broken, bloody dead body lying shattered in the rocky basin below.

I told myself, *Dying on a spiritual pilgrimage is an auspicious way to go — and death of the physical body is not the end — my spirit is infinite....* Even so, I was breathing through the fear as my gut felt like it already went over the cliff on the ascent. When I reached the slippery incline, my mule's hind legs slipped over the edge... WUMP...MY GUIDE WHACKED HIS LEGS BACK ON THE TRAIL.... My life was saved.

Later on the bus ride back through the foothills, we were chatting about the significance of my finger wound and how it happened while cutting *prasad* from AnandiMa. We thought it was a necessary sacrifice to clear the negative karma from my family lineage. I am thinking of Gandhi's seven dangers to human virtue — precept number seven — worship without sacrifice. I ponder the meaning of that. The discipline of sacrifice requires that we give up something of value for something else of greater value. Sacrifice challenges us to transform through effort, perseverance. Sacrifice strengthens our will, which strengthens our spiritual muscle. As we mature in our spiritual growth, it is a necessary force to withstand the gravitational pull of our negative thoughts and actions in our daily life. In this cultural age of the quick fix, sacrifice is not a popular experience. The effort of sacrifice is heroic in transcending the limitations of our daily life.

# 24. When a Great Being Dies

$T$o be loved unconditionally by someone leaves behind a clear grace and, yes, grief when the loved one departs through physical death or other circumstances. So it was for me when Dhyanyogi took Maha Samadhi in August 1994. It has been almost three decades since AnandiMa, Dileepji, fifty disciples, and myself had the unfathomable blessing to be in India at the time of Guruji's Mahasamadhi. What I experienced there was an initiation into the deeper mysteries of my own soul. The mystery to be pondered: What happens to the disciple when a great spiritual master dies?

Since the beginning of the trip and even before, I had a sense something extraordinary was about to happen, and that I had to be with Guruji no matter what—even at the cost of losing a very good job, since I couldn't take a leave of absence. In the few weeks before Guruji died, we were on pilgrimage to the Valley of Flowers and Hemkund in the Himalayas. From my observations, I could see we were all going through profound purifications at the physical and subtle levels. Within myself, I experienced a rapid ascent of spiritual energy that required me to use *sankalpa* and cease all spiritual practices to gain control of my energy, so that I could function in the activities of our pilgrimage. You could say that ascending and descending the Himalayas was going on in my soul.

The day before our arrival in Calcutta, AnandiMa, several disciples, and I began feeling a tugging energy at our heart. I can only describe this energy as a pulling outward of my *prana* (life force) and waves of grief, as if a part of me were dying.

We had just arrived in Calcutta, looking forward to a private meeting with Mother Theresa. In the early morning hours, AnandiMa received a phone call that Dhyanyogi took Maha

81

Samadhi. We cancelled our meeting with Mother Theresa. That evening, I woke up at 3:00 AM with an intense grief. I sat on the bathroom floor weeping for all the sadness I had ever lived. My grief was a clean grief. I had no issues for clearing personally with Dhyanyogi—just love that healed the repressed grief of a lifetime. To this day, I can no longer miss him for he has become the wisdom in my heart and the light of the divine in everything. I feel a tremendous peace.

Amidst confusion, shock, and grief, fifty disciples boarded India Airlines in the early morning to join AnandiMa and Dileepji, who were making preparations for the final *darshan* and ancient funeral rites of cremation in Ahmedabad, Gujarat. In the meditation hall at Hansol Ashram, we arrived to see Dhyanyogi looking magnificent in death, propped on a throne of ice, ready to receive his beloved disciples for the final *darshan*. More than once, many of us went up to Guruji and then AnandiMa to offer our grief, to bow and touch their feet according to the tradition in India to honor a spiritual master.

After *darshan*, the preparations of Guruji's body for cremation began. The boundaries of my ego having been blurred by lack of sleep and grief, I was completely in my heart. Sometimes I cried, sometimes I was beyond tears, beyond breath, mind, and time. This is what it must have been like to witness the burial rites of Christ and the ancient spiritual masters of other traditions. We were experiencing the sorrow and mystery of Christ's disciples and what all disciples throughout time experience when a beloved master passes beyond the physical plane of existence.

We all watched how, with great love and tenderness, disciples bathed, anointed Guruji's body with sacred perfume of sandalwood, and wrapped his body in a white shroud, while our bodies and the air around us vibrated with the recitation of the traditional ancient mantras for the soul's journey through death.

## Cremation

We followed as best we could behind the disciples carrying Dhyanyogi's body to be laid on the sandalwood pyre. While we walked, we chanted, as some of us were anointed by the sacred red *kumkum* powder being thrown on the procession. AnandiMa and Dileepji lit the pyre.

How can I bear this? It felt as if the doors of my heart had been broken open with everything exposed. Guruji's *prana* dissolving into the infinite. Guruji's body burning to ashes. My own heart being purified in the inner pyre. Did Guruji say a *sankalpa* before he died to hasten our purification and bring us closer to enlightenment? I was aware of AnandiMa's grief and how Guruji was everything to her. And my own feelings of love, gratitude, and protectiveness to her and Dileepji. A few of us stayed behind into the early morning hours until the burning of his body was finished.

By the morning, I had developed acute laryngitis. No sound, not even a peep or a whisper could come out. It was a blessing. For the next several days, I was completely immersed in the silence of Guruji. And he was everywhere in everything! Inside and outside. Guruji so loved birds. In his room lived a pigeon that he had a special relationship with. During those special days of profound purification and silence, one or two pigeons were almost always by the window in our hotel room. My roommate noticed it also. When I got off the elevator at different floors, they were there as well, outside of the window — Guruji sending messages of comfort.

For the ten days remaining of the trip, we rested, attended a memorial service for Guruji at Hansol Ashram, a *bhandara* in Guruji's name at a local temple, and a day trip to Bhandvad, Guruji's old ashram in the desert where AnandiMa lived when she was a girl. A small group of us stayed on after the trip was over. It was heartbreaking for our group to be separated after being so close in our grief.

## The Narmada River

Guruji wanted certain *puja* practices to be done in his name by a specific date at the Narmada River in Gujarat. We were worried about getting to the Narmada River in time because the countryside was flooded by the monsoon. Some prayers were offered and a few days before the deadline, the floods subsided. We were able to pass through.

A temple in a village along the Narmada River was chosen ahead of time for the *puja*. Getting there was an adventure by boat and on foot. The boat was an ancient construction of wood, cloth sail, bound together by rope—not a nail in sight and with enough space between the floorboards for some water to come in over our feet. Would we sink or swim to our destination? I was never quite sure.

Once on land, we then had a few kilometers to walk on flat, muddy lowlands to get to the village. With almost every step, our feet would sink into the mud over our ankles and make a loud sucking sound as the mud claimed our sandal upon extricating our foot. What a joke. Symbolic of our being stuck in the muck of Maya. Ha! After what seemed like hours of this, we were warmly received by some residents of the village with water to wash our feet and a wonderful meal before we left that day.

The *puja* ceremony was beautifully done in behalf of Guruji, to merge his *prana* with the Guru Universal Tattva. AnandiMa explained to us that traditionally, when someone dies, the puja is done to merge the prana with the parents, except if there is a guru. The final part of the *puja* was to put the offerings in the river. Our boat couldn't accommodate all of us. Some disciples were chosen. I was heartbroken to miss the last offerings. Another disciple and I followed behind the group and waited on the shore, while the others got on. At the last minute, AnandiMa said, "Come on." She is very much like a mother who knows what is in the heart of her children. We watched with love and gratitude, chanting while AnandiMa offered the puja—the sacred mantras, the ashes merging into the earth's prana, the sturdy coconut carrying the rice and flowers home over the waters. The river accepted with gladness while we watched the offering merge with the current in the late afternoon dusk.

## Bihar Province: A Visit to Guruji's Hometown

Guruji's grandnephews met us the airport. For the rest of our stay, they accompanied us and treated us like family. Guruji's hometown is a very small impoverished village in the countryside of Bihar. On our arrival, we had lunch at a relative's house, followed by a visit to the house Guruji was born in and a tour of the hospital he founded.

What a special blessing to be standing in the doorway of the house Guruji lived in as a boy. And in such humble circumstances! It was very simple—a dirt floor, a hearth, one long room for a large family of eight or nine children. Some old family pictures were still on the walls. No one lives there now but the family maintains it. Dileepji said, "the place where a great being is born is not important but the parents are."

Guruji's hospital was a size large enough for the needs of the village, with old but adequate equipment and the donated ambulance outside. We were sad to see the potential not being used, because the hospital had to be closed for lack of funds.

Before we returned to our hotel, a few of us interviewed some local doctors to become more knowledgeable about the hospital circumstances, in the hopes of having it operating again in the future. On the long bumpy ride home, I realized although it's good, important to do charitable works, those works are always subject to fluctuations of karma at the physical level of existence. The blossoming of the soul to God-realization goes beyond all that—the highest goal we can achieve as human beings.

## Bodhgaya, Bihar (Buddha's Place of Enlightenment)

In my memory now, I think of it as the place of flowers, although I can recall there not being anymore flowers there than other places in India. Our hotel was just a short walk to the Bodhi Tree where Buddha sat until he became enlightened. Our small group of disciples went there to meditate at sunset.

The tree was magnificent in its full-bodied majesty, surrounded by a fence in the courtyard of a temple. At dusk, bells rang for the silent meditation period. In my excitement at being blessed with the opportunity to meditate in this sacred place with my guru, my mind thought, *This is it! You're at the tree. Better hurry up and get enlightened now.* As I went into meditation, I could feel the waves of peaceful energy from the place as part of my own body and then a flood of really intense emotion. The heat had been on with me for the past couple of years, and the India trip was especially a time of great sensitivity. Dileepji reminded me, "It's just a phase. It will pass." I forget sometimes and needed to be reminded. AnandiMa went into *samadhi* very quickly under the Bodhi Tree. Every day, our group meditated at dusk under the Buddha's tree.

We returned to Ahmedabad to rest after our pilgrimage to Buddha's land. During that time, there was an outbreak of the bubonic plague in Surat, which was fifty kilometers from where we were staying. I thought it best to delay my return to the U.S. to avoid quarantine en route. That was a wise decision. After all I had been through on this trip, I was not psychologically prepared to integrate back into the American culture.

# Epilogue

Guruji's work continues to grow in the heart of the disciple. The hospital he established in Bihar has now reopened. AnandiMa and Dileepji with the love and support of disciples now bring Guruji's work to Europe and South America, as well as the U.S. and India. As for myself, I do have a new life. Having been in India at the time of Guruji's Maha Samadhi allowed me to move to a deeper level at a critical time in my spiritual evolution. The difficulty and pain I experienced there have also become bliss in my memory. Maybe pain and bliss are not so far apart after all.

My personal memory of Dhyanyogi is forever imprinted in my heart; there he was sitting in his room in silent Darshan, waves upon waves of Pure, Unconditional Love flowing from him, permeating every cell of my being. Another memory comes to mind again—of being twelve years old and wishing I could experience what Christ's disciples experienced, instead of reading about it in a book. That wish has been fulfilled in every way through Guruji and AnandiMa. Because of their grace, I can now experience the Guru Tattva as a living presence—formless and impersonal, yet intimate like the closest friend, almost continuously. I will always be thankful to the day I die for being at Guruji's Maha passing and for everything I experienced in India. The mystery of God.

The last time I saw him in his body, he told me when he was no longer in the body, he would guide me through my intuition. Only I wouldn't know it was him—I would think it was me. I share with you, beloved reader, one of the greatest pearls of Guruji's wisdom that keeps my ego in check in my enlightenment journey through life. I was describing my experiences of *samadhi* and my gratitude to the lineage, to

AnandiMa and Dileepji. I mentioned that now that I am experiencing almost continuous states of waking *samadhi*, I don't need to meditate anymore. They advised me, *"We're telling you what Guruji told us. Don't think you can't fall back out of that state. So long as you are in a human body, you can always fall back. You must always be vigilant. Never stop your spiritual practices. What you are experiencing is only the beginning."* My inflated ego popped.

Guruji's wise words have helped me through many egoic crises, especially during the later betrayal of a world-renowned healer who was a channel for miraculous healing. The greatest gift of his and AnandiMa's love set me free to live in love myself. May you who are reading this know this state of love. For those of you who already know it, may it grow exponentially. I wish you, dear reader, peace in your heart.

# 25. New Frontier

*I*n the fifteen years of my spiritual discipleship, I grew in my ability to enter deep states of meditation — *samadhi* — to experience bliss, peace, and communion with the divine within. My greatest desire was to be in this state every waking moment. I did not know how to do that. What got in the way? Can you guess?

My thoughts, which were negative more often than I desired. And my erratic Italian passionate emotions often got the best of my intentions. So what could I do? I asked myself the question, "What could be a quicker or more immediate way to be in the bliss and peace state in the moment that didn't require all this practice?" As usual, the unanswered question gained momentum parked in my heart. When we have a desire to know more, then the universal appreciation bank wants to make that happen for us. Ever notice that? It can take time, though.

Got to be patient. Every little blip of gratitude appreciates in the manifestation bank. Then it explodes when it builds up enough energy to become birthed into the physical reality of your life. You don't even have to worry about it. When you catch yourself in a negative thought, for instance, "I don't have enough money to buy that vacation," switch it around by imagining how great it feels to be on the vacation! You don't have to believe it in your mind — fake it. Let your feeling heart take care of the rest.

Where was I up until age forty-four, the biggest most transformative time of my life? I mentioned that I had a growing dissatisfaction with my life. I had started teaching meditation and yoga in 1995. At thirty-nine years, I gave birth to my son, Ian. I was also sculpting. As an older mom, I was very often tired from nurturing a baby. Yet, a quiet soul unrest was always there in the background. My spirit wanted to soar and expand beyond anything I had experienced before. Enlightened moments are a nonstatic state. The consciousness bands of enlightenment are infinite.

As I have said, these stealth desires have a way of popping up when we lease expect it or even want it. You ever notice how the biggest events in our life were the ones we never planned on? I felt dissatisfied with the mind-based meditation techniques I had grown accustomed to. Yet, I did feel sparks of connection to my heart when I went deep enough in meditation and felt bliss or peace. Internally, I asked the question, "Is there a faster way to go deeper in my meditation using my heart first? Is there anyone out there doing anything with the heart in this way? In the meditation classes I taught, I began teaching my students visualization exercises to deepen their heart connection as an aid to enter deeper into meditation. Several years went by....

In 1998, I had attended a lecture to help my son in his brain development—to provide for him through my parenting his needs to grow into a confident, creative happy child. The lecture turned out to be about the new science of the heart that brings balance and harmony in every cell, uniting spirit to mind and body, with the potential to heal every cell of the body to its original health in functioning. I had the ahaa moment—"That's what I want to study and practice!" I had the desire to help others with this connection. But what did I do? I said, "No. I have too much going on in my life."

Six months later, in a small library in Westbrook, Maine, I met an artist colleague I hadn't seen in over a decade. There were not very many people in the library, mind you—I don't even remember her name now. She started talking about the folks who were coming out with the heart techniques and science that the lecture was about. Again, I felt the desire to go for it and I said, "No. Not Now." I simply was not ready for such a commitment. Then the years went by and I had completely forgotten about the desire to learn more about the heart and the folks who were doing amazing work with the heart in the world.

# Part Two

# **Liberation**

# 26. There's Something Happening in Here...

*I*n 2000, I had begun experiencing these strange, mysterious symptoms. I was getting blinding headaches. The headaches were so bad I had trouble walking, my balance was off, and I would feel pressure behind my eyes and a black hole I could see blocking my vision. The headaches would come and go. A close health journalist friend said, "It sounds like brain tumor symptoms." What a horrible thought. A BRAIN TUMOR? When they want someone to die in a soap opera, they either give 'em a fatal car crash or a brain tumor! This can't be happening to me! So I went to my PCP doctor. She tested me with neurological exercises. Her diagnosis was that I was a middle-aged, hormonal, stressed out, out of shape woman. I taught yoga, mind you. She gave me a prescription for migraine medication.

My husband and I got a second opinion at the medical center and the doctors agreed with my doctor's diagnosis. We even asked, "Do you think I have a brain tumor? Do you think I need a CAT scan?"

"No. No," they said. The symptoms mysteriously subsided for several months in the summer of 2000.

By fall, the headaches started becoming worse—I was taking large doses of Tylenol and Ibuprofen to deaden the pain—to no relief. The symptoms and the fear drove me to see my doctor yet again. She said that the headaches were being caused by my addiction to Tylenol and Ibuprofen. I was to go off them.

I had a premonition *something really horrible was going to happen to me.* Our spirit does its best to guide us and will use whatever it takes to get our attention. I had a dream in which I was about to get out of my car parked in my driveway. Suddenly, out of the yard, came a gigantic white wolf. He pressed his nose against my window and kept tap, tap, tapping his nose. The great white wolf's eyes locked on mine. I became scared and woke up! I knew I was visited by a divine animal who was trying to tell me about something. It felt like a warning that my life was in danger.

In another dream: I was walking down a corridor and the walls and ceiling started closing in around me. I woke up before I was crushed. This was a reoccurring nightmare. I was scared there was something the matter with me—I was dying and I didn't know what from. The panic I felt was slow and seeping— I could keep it at bay through spiritual practice that also helped me cope with the pain from the headaches.

In my desperation, I got reconnected with my Celtic spiritual teacher in Massachusetts. She gave me an updated numerology reading in November of 2000. "A significant event is going to happen in March that will liberate you. It will take several years for you to integrate the experience."

Back in Maine, I sought divine counsel in meditation. I heard the still small voice inside say, *"Yes, something is going to happen. You will be allowed to live."* That didn't comfort me much—"to be allowed to live," meant it was something life-threatening with a lot of suffering. I prayed for strength and courage.

# 27. It Happens...

*I*n February of 2001, the headaches came back in fuller, even more intensity. I could barely admit to myself much less communicate to my family and friends the gnawing desperation the headaches brought on. My husband left for Florida to be with his brother and left me to care for our five-year-old son Ian. My strength of will helped me to function in the first week alone with Ian. Yet my strength of will could only go so far. My strength, refuge, and comfort would have to come from God.

Ian so loves his caregiver family, Darlene, Vanessa, and Vance. On the weekend I left Ian in their care and went to a local convent for a spiritual retreat by the sea in Biddeford, Maine. Alone with God, I knew the life threatening event was imminent. In the sanctuary of my room overlooking the ocean, I offered special mantras and prayers asking God to spare my life. Although I didn't know what the event was—I prayed and made a list of everything I wanted to live for and wanted to do that I hadn't done. Once again the animal world came to warn me through the swarm of crows circling outside my window. They told me the event would happen within seven days.

## *The Convent Chapel*

I am praying for my life on the hard wooden bench. I wish that the suffering that is upon me would go away. I am so afraid! *Please, God, take this away from me!* I notice the sunlight filtering through the stained glass, illuminating the large wooden cross over the altar. I am reminded of Christ's passion of suffering. I understand. May this unavoidable event take me to a level of transformation in love that I have never experienced before.

## Sunday, February 25, 2001

I was thankful that the headaches, dizziness and vertigo were manageable enough for me to drive myself home from the retreat center. By the time I parked my car and rested my head on the steering wheel, I knew I was not capable of parenting Ian alone.

On the phone with Darlene, "My symptoms are getting worse. I was barely able to drive myself home. Will you take in Ian?"

"Yes of course!"

"And Darlene? I don't want to worry him. Tell him Mama just needs a little more rest."

"Don't worry. He'll be fine. I'm coming over tomorrow to take you to emergency."

On Monday in the emergency room at Maine Medical Center, I was not given an X-ray, but given medication and told to go back to my PCP doctor.

## Tuesday

My doctor the next day gave me Imitrex injections, with the same diagnosis about being stressed out and out of shape. On Thursday, the pain was so bad—I gave the injections. They didn't work and I could no longer walk and see very well. From my bed, I called 911 and was carried out by ambulance.

This now being my second time in emergency since Monday, the doctor who attended me read my report and said, "I am a mother, and I have a mother's intuition that you need a CAT scan." Meanwhile, the doctor with the intuition tracked down my brother-in-law in Florida, who was a police detective with an unlisted number, to inform my husband about my emergency situation.

The CAT scan revealed a very large frontal lobe bilateral meningioma brain tumor. When I looked into the eyes of the doctor who was to be my neurosurgeon, I felt a flash of recognition. Having recall of many past lives—the flashback was that he was a significant karmically prepared person from a long ago warrior lifetime as an American Indian, to remove the tumor now—very significant—it had to be him. Interesting to note after seeing me through the first year of recovery, my neurosurgeon moved back to New Mexico after having practiced just a year and a half in Maine. His spiritual connection and heart was homesick for the Native American community he served in a clinic there.

I was kept in the hospital, treated with drugs to prepare me for emergency surgery on Monday. How does one prepare for the possibility of one's own death in four days? At least I had time, though. I signed off on my life and that I did not want my life to continue if I could not breathe on my own. I planned my funeral with my closest friend. My family and friends set up a worldwide prayer team.

In the precious little time I had to adjust to the diagnosis— possible death by one or more strokes in the surgery—and the knowledge that the structural and cognitive changes that would happen to my brain as a result of the surgery could be permanent. As I was facing the possibility of my own death, I was also thinking, *What's it going to be like if I live? Isn't brain intelligence everything, what we rely on, what we know? What if my cognitive function is so severely impaired I can no longer do spiritual practices?* I went into surgery reciting the *Maha Mrityunjaya* death-defying mantra.

## *Maha Mrityunjaya Mantra*

*Om Tryambakam Yajaamahe*
*Sugandhim Pussttivardhanam*
*Urvaarukamiva Bandhanaan*
*Mrtyormukssiiya Maamrtaat*

**Meaning:**
Om, We Worship the Three-Eyed One (Lord Shiva),
Who is Fragrant and who Nourishes all beings.
May He Liberate us from fear of Death, for the
sake of Immortality,
Even as a ripe Cucumber is severed from the
Bondage of the creeper.

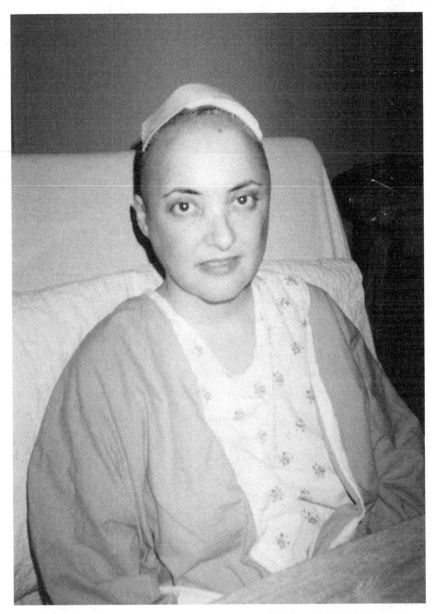

Jasmina, recovery post surgery March 7, 2001

# 28. The Surgery

*I* didn't leave my body in consciousness—hover over it in the operation room, like near-death experiences you may have read or heard about. I left completely...I entered a tunnel and kept falling and falling in complete blackness, nothingness. I felt trust, letting go completely in the falling.... There were divine beings who were around me, protecting me, their illuminated hands guiding me through the darkness in the falling. I came to a great light, a light bright like the sun, yet soft and soothing as moonlight.

In front of the light was my spiritual master, Dhyanyogi, who had left the body in Maha Samadhi in 1994. When a student took initiation in his spiritual lineage, he promised he would accompany our soul to meet God at the time of our bodily death.

He was there before me now in a beautiful, radiant, holographic pattern of light. I said to him telepathically, "I want to go into that light and then I want to come out, back into my body and live."

He said, "Yes, I will help."

I went into the light. My memory is spotty. I remember going in front of an assembly of divine light beings whose grace enveloped me. In their presence from my higher self, I assessed my life and previous lives. I found I needed to love myself and others more and that my mission would be revealed to me. It was my own judgment day, not in a court with a stern judge passing sentence, but from the highest source of soul discernment, in the loving witness presence of the divine light assembly. I can be very sensitive to feeling judged by someone. There was no shame in my soul assessment of my imperfections—only joy at the greater opportunity to become more love.

I woke up in the recovery room with the bright white light around me and speaking words of love for my husband. The light stayed with me for all the months of acute recovery, March 5, 2001 – June, 2001.

Because the light illuminated me, I looked and acted better than I really was. On my third day of recovery in the hospital, the doctors on my team sent me home and took me off the seizure medications. Within three days at home, my condition rapidly deteriorated—I had three seizures due to the brain swelling and I could no longer stand or walk. Seizures short-circuit the nervous system so much that the fatigue is disabling. I was given large doses of seizure meds to control them. Although the seizure meds have very heavy side effects, they were necessary to stabilize my brain to do its healing.

A day after the seizures, while lying in bed in a very weakened condition, I was in the light, yet aware of my surroundings. I spoke to my sister who was taking care of me, "I am going to do this work with the heart and help others. I will need to study and the money will come to me to do that." She looked at me wistfully—unbelieving how all that could be with my present state of deterioration.

For the months of acute recovery, I often prayed in a real way. After all, God is our best friend, which means we can get REAL. My prayer would go something like this: "Look, if you want me to do this heart work, then give me a complete recovery. GIVE ME MY BRAIN BACK."

# 29. Acute Recovery

*I*n acute recovery, learning how to walk wasn't the only challenge to my injured brain. I had speech and language challenges, short-term memory, emotional trauma, and attention issues to spice up my recovery. The pain of recovery was beyond any kind of sanity. I lay in bed in a darkened room. My eyes couldn't tolerate light. My mind was unraveling, hallucinating from the powerful drugs I was on to control the seizures and the head pain. All I could do was breathe in the light. The consciousness state of the light took me in the moment out of identification with the experience of suffering. "I am not this body, these hallucinating thoughts, these fear emotions."

The side effects of the drugs kept me from sleeping for long periods of time. For the first two months, I would sleep for one and a half to two hours at a time. I knew when every streetlight would come on at different times throughout the night. I tried to not panic and remain detached when I heard inside my head, a radio station announcing the local weather in Bangor, one hundred eighty miles away from my bedside...and visual hallucinations...like living inside a surreal Hieronymus Bosch painting—the barriers in my mind of memory, time and place unleashed.

All the years of spiritual practice prepared me to cope with suffering beyond anything I had ever imagined I could live through. This high state of mindful awareness helped me view my experience with detachment, which protected me from the abyss of insanity. This state of consciousness became my haven and home, and shielded me from over identifying with my debilitated condition.

# 30. My Miracle Heart

*I* began noticing that my heart was playing an important role in my recovery. Being so depleted in my left-brain functions left my intuitive right brain free to expand. I literally could see inside my body, brain, and heart. I noticed when I felt gratitude for my life, for the birds singing outside my window, the sun shining onto my bed, I saw my heart light up, the light flowing up into my brain—calming and helping me to focus better. My injured brain was so sensitive to stress, that when I was frustrated, sad, or depressed about my condition and the effects it was having on my family, it could bring on a seizure, cause mental confusion, and exacerbate my brain injury symptoms.

The emotional trauma I experienced on a daily basis was unlike anything I had ever encountered. I called it my daily trauma date, 7:30—9:00 AM. I would cry and shake as the waves of trauma emotions passed through my body and spirit. Our connection to our heart is natural. I knew intuitively that my heart was guiding the release of trauma.

Beloved reader, what I was experiencing was an initiation into the healing power of the spiritual heart. When we are in what I call *heart time*, we are in the now, where all emotionally traumatic memories can be cleared. In the now, we can both clear the past and create the future.

When we bring our body, mind, and emotions in sync through a special process I can teach you, using intention, breath, and a positive or spiritual emotion, we enter *Heart Time*.

The healing effect of clearing a traumatic emotional memory in *heart time*, ricochets throughout time—past, present, and future. We now have a new foundation to attract more abundance, joy and fulfillment in our life. It can be very supportive and in some situations very necessary to have the help of a qualified spiritual coach, therapist or healer in this process. We are not alone. Universal consciousness is a living breathing reality of light, designed to attract to us the love and support we need.

As my heart guided me in the release of trauma emotions in my recovery, I felt better, more peaceful until the next series of trauma waves came up. Healing the dis-ease in our soul is a spiraling process over our entire life.

My trauma dates occurred for six months post surgery. I am thankful my neurologist didn't recommend meds for the anxiety and trauma emotions, because that would have interfered with the natural trauma clearing my body needed. Just a word of caution here: If you need meds, that is okay, too. You can still heal emotionally from trauma. Our bodies have their own wisdom when we take the time to listen to it.

I noticed how sensitive I was to my environment. The people I wanted to have around me were those who had a peaceful, loving, positive attitude. The last thing I wanted was to be influenced by a worrying attitude, which would frighten me and cast doubt on my faith that I was healing in a miracle way.

Oh, I shall never forget how lifesaving community support was to my family and my recovery. At times in my life, I had stealth thoughts I would only allow myself to contemplate late at night: *What if something catastrophic happened to my family and me? Would I be abandoned and homeless with my family?* Those thoughts were so scary I could barely admit to them. And when the catastrophic situation of the brain tumor happened, the community became our safety net.

My dear friend, Darlene, my sister Debbie, the local church community, and my son's kindergarten teacher rallied to help with food, my medical care, and physical therapy. My son was taken care of by Darlene and the church community. When my self-employed husband couldn't work because he needed to care for me around the clock, relatives and friends donated money. I had a personal care attendant, a physical and occupational therapist come to my home. I experienced an outpouring of love from the community that I can only repay by paying it forward. Every kind thought, word, and deed matters in ways we cannot imagine.

My five-year-old son, Ian, would come home from school to be my brain game guy. I had to monitor the fatigue and plan my day accordingly so that I would have the energy to do the activities I loved best. Best of all was sitting up in bed with my son and playing the Concentration Game with cards—Ha, my son and I were both improving our memory! His was much better. With a delicious bowl of ice cream, we enjoyed other simple games like Chutes and Ladders to get those executive functions jump-started. There is plenty of scientific research that supports our brains really can reconnect its synapses after an injury.

A big lesson for me was to ask for help and support. Being the shy introvert that I am, that was not easy. One such time, Ian needed a ride to a private school out of our town. I was not able to drive on seizure meds. I tried to get public assistance to get him a ride. Bus service is not good in Maine from town to town.

After calling many agencies to get assistance, I started to come apart emotionally, which always exacerbated my recovery fatigue symptoms. Each agency would refer me to the next. I completely broke down on the phone with a receptionist. While weeping, I told her my predicament. She let me know right away she couldn't help me with a ride. In empathy she continued, "I know what you're going through. I recovered from a stroke. My family would get impatient with me. You are going to be well. It will be okay." Her encouragement was food for my fatigued brain and spirit. I felt better about myself. As it turned out, an acquaintance of a teacher in Ian's school gave him rides to school. We just had to pay for gas. You know the old bible saying, "Ask and ye shall receive."

Maybe it's our upbringing that encourages us to be ashamed of asking for and receiving help. For the first time in my life, I was begging for help. It was not how can I help you, but how can you help me? Receiving is as important as giving. If we let ourselves get so depleted from giving that the well runs dry— we cannot give to others except our own thirst for care. People feel that nonverbally when we allow our well to run dry, then resentment is projected outward to taint the care we are offering. I learned to take time to reaffirm my gifts, my divine connection through meditation, prayer, and doing activities that gave me joy and feelings of belonging.

# 31. Heart Training

$G$uess what? You know that premonition I had with my sister in my early recovery after I had the seizures? Well, eight months into my recovery in September 2001, I met a man who unintentionally guided me to the folks with the scientific heart techniques that made an impression on me years ago and that I had forgotten about.

One afternoon, the man came into my office at the yoga center with his resume, hoping to coteach my meditation class. At that time, I was well enough to teach a yoga and meditation class once a week. Inside his resume was an article from a yoga magazine advertising HeartMath®'s scientifically based heart centered stress management techniques and technology. In a flash my mind lit up with the memory. That's it! They're the folks I wanted to study with in 1998. They're the ones who will help me unfold my heart healing mission that was revealed to me in the near death experience of my brain surgery recovery. Even so, being the cautious turtle that I am, I waited two weeks to be sure I was ready to take the next step, before calling the HeartMath number and saying "yes" to the call of destiny.

I trained with HeartMath by first developing my own case history of experience. Even though I had intuitively sensed and had begun using the power of my heart, the HeartMath folks' techniques were simple, direct, easy to apply, and produced results quickly in the moment. I can tell you in brain injury recovery that is no small accomplishment.

In my early recovery, if someone talked fast, I couldn't understand a word they were saying. And English is my first and only language. The brain heals slowly over time. To retain new information, I had to read slowly and go over my material more than one time. I was someone who had a photographic memory as an adult, remembering long passages of poems and information. Brain injury recovery was like being an adult baby overnight. A real tweak to my ego identity that likes to be in control and prided for my intelligence.

Beloved readers, I was learning another kind of intelligence: heart intelligence, or what some folks refer to as emotional or spiritual intelligence. I refer to it as miracle heart. Don't let your mind fool you as to the reality of the power of the miracle heart. We intuitively sense our heart connection. Just think of all the mysterious references we have about our hearts, from many cultures, spiritual traditions, and philosophers. Now, scientific research has proven what we already knew deep down inside our hearts. The light I saw from my heart flowing upwards to sooth and calm my brain in acute recovery, is indeed one of the ways the heart communicates to the brain through the autonomic nervous system. (To find out more about the amazing power of the heart, go to Hearmath.org.)

I had a client who was a dedicated bible reader. She would come to her sessions with me and read all the heart references from the bible. I was astounded there were so many. And then there was the client who the last thing she would be doing was read from any bible. I couldn't say any reference to anything spiritual or even use the word.

She started practicing the heart techniques and feeling the power connection inside. We didn't call it God—it was her energy of well-being. She even had trouble believing it with her mind until her miracle heart showed her. She started seeing heart symbols everywhere.... One time, she stepped onto her walkway and there on the ground was a triple heart image engraved in mud in a puddle after a rainstorm. She gifted me with the photo that I have in my office. Another time, she found a fall leaf at her feet with a heart shape that nature carved into the leaf. She laminated the leaf as a heart souvenir.

Sometimes, a person can be so wounded that they cannot connect to their heart and help heal themselves. So what do we do? We love them. Just showing kindness creates a coherent field of love that affects their entire physiology. HeartMath® has done some wonderful research proving the effects that positive emotions have on people and animals.

We never know when we will be called upon to show love to someone and what the circumstances may be.... March 2002, my family and I boarded the Delta Flight from Portland, Maine to Fort Lauderdale, Florida, looking forward to a break from the long harsh winter in Maine. I felt especially wonderful and hopeful. I had been practicing using the power of my heart with HeartMath's techniques and experiencing the extraordinary effect it was having on all aspects of my brain injury recovery from the surgery a year ago in March. I was in the process of developing the case study of my progress to send to the director of scientific research at the Institute of HeartMath. I was studying and practicing to become licensed to coach others in applying HeartMath's techniques for personal well-being.

We got comfortable in our seat in the economy section, my husband seated in the middle, my son at the window, and myself on the aisle seat. I couldn't help but listen in on the conversation from the woman sitting in front of me to the woman at the window seat. The middle seat was empty. "I have anxiety attacks on airplanes at takeoff and landing." The window seat woman instructed her on abdominal breathing, which she was familiar with from Lamar's training, to offset the anxiety.

I thought, *H-m-mm. My training in HeartMath's techniques indicated that fear can be further locked into the solar plexus with abdominal breathing. The heart has to be engaged through breath and positive feeling to fully release the fight or flight response in the body and mind. Okay. I hope the abdominal breathing works for her.*

The plane starts ascending. The woman in front of me cries out, "It's happening!" She tries the abdominal breathing. "It's not working." She starts shaking. I have an internal dialogue with myself—*I want to help her. Should I do it? What will my husband and the other people think if it doesn't work? I'll embarrass myself.* Understand, dear readers, I am a somewhat shy, introverted New Englander. I notice the other passengers' reactions of fear to her anxiety attack. Airplanes these days are not the calmest places to be. *No time left gotta act now.* I lean forward and touch her arm. "Can I help you?" She cannot speak. She is holding her breath, shaking and turning a deep shade of red tinged with blue. She nods *YES.*

In a soft, firm voice, I talked her through to connect with her heart with some simple steps. Within sixty seconds, she came out of the anxiety attack. She remained calm for the rest of the flight. At landing, she needed a refresher to reconnect with her heart. I never knew her name.

We literally are broadcasting all the time either a coherent energy of positive feeling or fear. Even the more subtle negative emotions like judging someone who we think is in the wrong creates a stress response in the body. It's either one or the other. You can't have it both ways. Imagine what the world would be like if we just could get detached enough to notice what kind of signal we were sending out. When we take just a little more self-responsibility for our thoughts and emotions, we set the stage for the unlimited potential of miracles to happen in our lives.

*I invite you to take a moment with me now. What makes it hard for us to recognize and admit to our stress reactions is because we feel we*

*have done wrong. When we feel that, we end up repressing the emotion. Just pause. Take a breath with me. Close your eyes. Remember the last time someone was kind to you. Breathe that feeling in and hug yourself. Put your arms around yourself. It's that important to give love and acceptance to yourself.*

Every day I encourage you, and I am with you in spirit—just sit and breathe an attitude of compassion to yourself. Compassion is the doorway to forgiveness. To turn the key to unlock the forgiveness door, we have to be willing to let go of whatever or whoever caused our hurt or maybe something we did to someone else or a situation. We allow ourselves to let go—give it over and bring in compassion and let it soak in the heart. Understanding comes later—but first, compassion. Forgiveness and compassion are the most healing frequencies on our planet at this time. When we evolve more into the ability to use compassion, then unimaginable miracle manifestations will unfold for all of us.

# 32. New Normal

*O*ver several years, the result of all those heart practices gave me a miraculous recovery from the brain tumor surgery beyond the medical expectations. Anything that could make me feel better in the moment while I recovered was a miracle. How did I do this? I had what I refer to as my healing template. I saw myself as already whole and healed. The condition of my body, mind, and emotions are not who I really am. I am an infinite being of love, joy, compassion, whole and complete. I visualized and felt myself in this state of wholeness. The impression of our physical body exists as an original energetic template. I was using my intention bringing that energetic template into my physical template—my brain to rewire it. I did this by bringing in the positive emotions or spiritual frequencies in through my heart, along with visualizing and feeling my wholeness. Throughout this healing process, I did not know what kind of recovery I would get. I just kept focusing in the now, reaffirming that I am already healed.

Another very important aspect of heart consciousness I used was "soft heart," or tenderness, the kind of care you have for a suffering child or pet. I was often impatient with myself for all the cognitive deficits, the days when I barely had the energy to perform the simplest tasks to care for myself and my family, the days when trying to function with the migraine headaches. In those days, I stayed focused in soft heart, breathing the attitude of tenderness. It got me out of blame and feeling sorry for myself and helped me heal and just do the best I could for that day. The best for any given day was not the same day- to-day. "Soft heart" practice brought a feeling of acceptance, merciful compassion, and healing.

After only two months of very intensive practice using the miracle heart frequency of compassion, with the help of my HeartMath coach, David, I had the following dream: As *the late afternoon sun cast a soft golden glow in the living room of my home, I looked down the dark hallway to see, coming towards me, illuminated in an other worldly light, myself as a three year old. It was eerie seeing myself so illuminated, so real, standing at the entrance to the hallway. I looked like the image of a little girl Snow White — glowing fair skin, red cheeks, pixie style dark hair, and sparkling, large, dark eyes. She was glowing with pride and joy at her beautiful yellow dress. My little Snow White self said to me, "Do you want to see my new dress?"*

*"Oh, yes. I very much want to see your new dress."*

*"I'll show you," she said with unabashed enthusiasm, as she began twirling around and around. The yellow dress had the most beautiful white petticoat that gave the dress a full fluffy lift as my three year old self danced round and round, lifting her arms up and down like wings. Abruptly, the dancing stopped.*

*"Do you like it?"*

*"You look so-o-o beautiful in that dress. And you dance wonderfully!"*

*In a flash of yellow she jumped into my arms, wrapping her little girl arms and legs tightly around me in a joyful embrace. I held her securely, tenderly. "I love you," we said in unison. Bound together we laughed and cried as we twirled.* When I awoke, I lingered a long time in bed, weeping tears of love and acceptance.

After three months of heart practice, my neurosurgeon noticed how rapidly I was improving. "Whatever you are doing you are doing better than expected. It's going to be important if you hope to stay off the seizure meds, to manage your stress for the rest of your life. So go for it. Rewire your brain. Get it all back." My neurosurgeon soon moved back to New Mexico where his heart was. Like I mentioned before, he did his karmic deed for me and then went back home. I am blessed by him.

I did get it all back, with a few reminders. I got control of the seizures and the chronic post surgery headaches to stay off meds to this day, all of the cognitive deficits rewired to a new normal — to live in a state of gratitude and joy and to value my life every day. It's a ratio game you see. Through the heart, we can experience enlightened moments that grow and grow — it's a never-ending game. Don't expect it to end with you winning because it's not supposed to. That's why we humans are here, to experience our imperfection so we can grow in love, peace, and joy.

## 2005

So life went on for me. As a HeartMath coach, I had a growing client practice in Maine called HeartMath® for Health and Happiness and an affiliation with the True North Functional Medicine Center and helped many folks. One of the dearest desires of my heart was to help folks challenged to recover from brain injuries. With that desire, I worked with a compassionate holistic psychiatrist, Dr Rick Leskowitz, who helped me work with a brain injury support group in Boston at the Spaulding Rehabilitation Center. When I needed to rent an office in Boston to see clients from the support group, I prayed about it. I quickly got a very inexpensive office room in a beautiful pink Victorian building in Brookline, in a great neighborhood. Pink is a heart color by the way.

I commuted from Brookline to Maine for research in HeartMath® techniques and technology affecting TBI. That was an adventure in witnessing the miracles of resilience, courage, and perseverance in working with folks recovering from very debilitating brain injuries. I discovered: Even with a severe brain injury, so long as the function of *Will* is intact, folks can make the heart connection to change their heart rhythms to more peace, balance and harmony to affect all aspects of recovery.

All the commuting took its toll on my marriage. In the years after my surgery, I thought somehow that my experience of the light and living it in my recovery and helping my family would bring my husband and me closer together. Instead, my spiritual growth in heart consciousness created a wider gap that was there since my first trip to India in 1988.

I wanted it so much to not be so. And there was nothing I could do to stop it. We even went to counseling for two and a half years, and our counselor didn't think we had a lot in common, except to parent our son, Ian, to the best of our ability. We were both alone in the marriage, the stress of which was felt by Ian — what we consciously could not admit to ourselves.

# 33. Adrift

## 2007 Summer

*O*ur next-door neighbors had a church in their home. We were invited to their daughter's birthday party. Sitting across from me at our table was a young African American nineteen-year-old man. He kept looking at me intently even as we casually talked. He got up from the table abruptly and then came back with the minister's wife. She said, "This young man is our prophet. He saw something he needs to tell you."

The prophet and I went back to meet privately in the minister's office. I was a little uneasy because I feared what he might say. He said, "I was told to give you this message: Whatever you do, you must not have the surgery. You must pray to Christ to take this away from you—to completely heal you so you don't have to have the surgery. Only Christ can take this away from you. Do you know what this is about?"

I said, "No. I do not."

He reaffirmed, "This is the message I got."

I left the office and returned to the party even more uneasy. *Could it be that the tumor is growing back? God, no. Don't let it be so.*

## October

I am having lunch at Whole Foods with a friend from my intuition support group. We casually talk about healer colleagues we know. My friend says, "Oh, by the way, I recently went for a healing session with Harold! He is a very powerful energy healer and he has an institute in the U.S. He has been known to cure diseases and tumors."

I thought, *That's interesting*, a little uneasy in the back of my mind remembering the prophet's message. I said to my friend,

"I feel really good. I don't need a healer because I am in good health. But I will keep him in mind if I have the need in the future."

## 2008 January

It was time for my three-year MRI, which has always been negative—no tumor growth. This time, the MRI revealed a tumor the size of a lentil had started regrowing. My doctor advised radiation or surgery. With my TBI background, I knew I would not have the quality of brain intelligence to live a full, thriving, successful life if I chose either option. Besides, I knew in my heart that I could not live through the surgery, the prophet's message making every hair stand on end in my body.

I was in a state of emotional shock and desperation. I put out an SOS to the universe. *I want a miracle. Give me a miracle.* I did the only thing I knew to do for myself—to bring the light in through my heart to every cell of my body. I prayed for help. I knew that the help had to come from a greater collective healing energy force through others that I could not do on my own.

I waited and did my best to manage the fear thoughts that surfaced day-to-day. It was better to catch them when they first came up than to let them take me fully down the road to hopelessness and despair. I did my best to maintain a positive attitude to ease the worry of my son and husband.

Over the year, I got in touch with the healer, Harold, whom my friend had raved about. He canceled three consecutive sessions. It rattled my nerves—*it was not meant to be.* Then God, *what's next?* I silently whispered in my heart. I told myself to keep hope and trust and faith....

## April

My friend Mary and I are having breakfast after an intense workout at Curves. She knew I was living with the uncertainty of the regrowth of the brain tumor. "Mary, I am feeling this weird detachment from everyone, except Ian. It reminds me of the detachment from my body and my life that I experienced during the critical time after my brain surgery. It's like my emotional and physical energy is starting to withdraw. In early recovery, I was very aware that I could easily cross over into death. It's like I am saying goodbye to my life. Does this mean I am going to die soon?"

Like a true, caring, empathetic friend, Mary listened without judgment. I had asked a question that had no answer.

## *October*

We were at our intuition group meeting at the house of my friend, Darlene, in Westbrook. A friend reported that many folks were experiencing miraculous healings through a healer she had recently been to at Omega Institute. *I knew instantly. This is the master healer I am meant to see.* He had a healing center in South America. *I knew he would call me to come to his healing center.* I sent my photo through his guides. Two weeks later, I received a letter of invitation. The master healer invited me to his center for in-depth healing sessions. My guides said, "Out of fifty-seven photos that were brought to the healer, only you and another person were requested to come to the center."

At the time I received this message, I had returned to my marriage, after living with a friend who kindly offered her living space for me to destress, to think it through, to give it one more try. I was unprepared for the level of grief I had at leaving the marriage when I fled to my friend's home for refuge. Within the one-month period of returning to my husband, a deeper realization blasted its way to the light.

The truth of my marriage struck me like two strokes of lightning overnight. In a flash, I saw it all: John's unresolved substance abuse issues that undermined his confidence and took his spirit away from his family and work, the stress of coping with the changes in me and in our life after my brain tumor surgery, our lack of common shared interests and philosophies other than parenting our son. Our marriage was a sinking boat. We could bail the water out but not plug the holes.

If I could just stop being me, really settle down, stop being so selfish and calm my restless, expansive creative spirit. For several years, we had been living in limbo...just when did he start becoming emotionally abusive treating me like I had no feelings? And when did I stop caring—becoming indifferent and withdrawn? We reached the apex of the potential of our marriage. We could no longer grow together, only apart. We were at a permanent stalemate.

The truth of the second stroke of lightning frightened me to my core. I heard the still small voice of my heart whisper, *If you stay in this marriage, you will shorten your life.* In trying to save my marriage, I was trying to change my creative restless spirit. And my creative restless spirit was turning on me through illness, pining away for the unlived life.

I then knew within every cell of my being my marriage could not be saved. If I wanted to have the miracle healing, I needed to completely change my life. I did the only thing left to do, which was to leave my marriage for good. I didn't expect or know how deep the wound of grief I would have at letting go of the marriage and leaving my son with his dad.

Ian and his dad have had a deep, caring father-son relationship since his birth. How could I get in the way of that? Home is where the heart is. And Ian's home was with his dad, his school, his friends, and the loving church community.

Ian told me himself some time after I was settled in my new life. "I have had to grow up more after you left Papa and me. I am becoming a man and I need to be with a man—Papa. I don't mean to hurt your feelings, but that's the way it is."

Divorce can be as it has been said before—worse than burying a loved one. The person you are grieving is still alive living their life, and so you get a constant reminder. Someday, our society will be just as mindful of the support we need and don't get. How can we be expected to be married to one person for life when we have more than one life to live in this very one? Everyone—the whole family, relatives, and friends—needs the support. My relatives were not supportive. A few close friends were, and I let them help me with emotional support and moving into my new apartment.

# 34. The Apartment

*November 2008.*

$T$he orange curtains, the bright red couch. I craved the colors to help ground me, give me confidence in my shaky self-esteem and to dare to create a new life alone. I've always wanted to live in an *ashram* setting. This apartment became my *ashram* — two small rooms. Adequate. I surrounded myself with spiritual protection and covered the walls with the pictures of saints and spiritual masters. I fell asleep at night, safe in the imaginary arms of the saints and sages.

I pared down all my possessions to the essentials. I felt lighter in spirit all the way down to my body size. Years of excess weight began falling away. A whole new woman, a whole new life starting over in a new incarnation. The big difference is I didn't have to die to do it — I get to have all of my memories to both haunt and inspire me.

I haven't had to live alone and fend for myself for over twenty-eight years. How would I support myself? My coaching practice didn't fully support all my living expenses. I couldn't handle the stress of finding another job. Looming in the back of my mind was the brain tumor diagnosis, knowing that however I created the means to support myself in the next few years, it could all be blown away through illness. In the meantime, I attended the meetings and saw the clients from the medical center.

I will say the loneliness, the worry and anxiety drove me to learn how to knit. I couldn't meditate too much in my emotional state; knitting kept me calm enough to function. In the evening, the best I could do was sit, breathe, and knit. I have yet to finish the knitting of that shawl. What do you think I'm waiting for?

When I'm done, I plan to donate it to someone who needs it more than me.

Within two weeks after moving into my apartment, a divine synchronistic event occurred. My spiritual master, Sri AnandiMa, came back into my life with a sculpture commission to put a metallic golden patina finish on three life-size memorial brass sculptures of Sri Dhyanyogi. The commission took me to India to put the patina finish on the statue of my beloved spiritual master at her *ashram* in Nikora, Gujarat, India.

The money from the commission enabled me to live very frugally for three months until money came in from a pre-divorce settlement. During this time, our financial advisor called and said, "Guess what? You are losing money fast. What do you want to do with what's left?" *Whatever it takes* to live in peace, joy, health, and abundance became a call to use the money for that purpose.

OM SHRI MATRE NAMAHA
Salutations to the sacred Mother

OM BHAYA PAHAYAI NAMAHA
Salutations to the Mother who dispels all fear

OM NISHCHINTAYAI NAMAHA
Salutations to the Mother who is free from all anxiety

OM NIRMOHAYAI NAMAHA
Salutations to the Mother who is completely
free of delusion

OM NIHSAMSHAYAYAI NAMAHA
Salutations to the Mother who is free from doubt

OM NIRABADHAYAI NAMAHA
Salutations to the Mother who remains
ever untroubled

OM BHEDA NASHINYAI NAMAHA
Salutations to the Mother who destroys the distinctions made
by the mind

OM NIRAPAYAYAI NAMAHA
Salutations to the Mother who never departs

OM NIRATYAYAYAI NAMAHA
Salutations to the Mother who is beyond all danger

OM DUKHA HANTRYAI NAMAHA
Salutations to the Mother who destroys sorrow

OM SANDRA KARUNAYAI NAMAHA
Salutations to the Mother who is intensely compassionate

OM NIRVIKALPAYAI NAMAHA
Salutations to the Mother who is the eternal pure intelligence

*— From the 108 names of Divine Mother*

*Sri Yantra Temple* by the Narmada River at Sri
AnandiMa's Nikora Ashram, in Gujarat

## 35. Mother India rescues me...

*M id-January 2009.* Mumbai, the last time you engulfed me
with your teeming chaotic presence was in November, 1994,
after the bubonic plague outbreak in Surat. I remember leaving
you at dawn in the short ride by taxi through the metropolis of
traffic to the airport. I watched with a nostalgic longing as I
gazed at the orange pink sunrise, knowing deep down that it
would be perhaps many years or not at all would I ever return
to you....

How good it was to be back, alive in the crowded womb of
life and death in Mumbai. I am not the bravest, most
independent traveler. In my travels, I seldom travel alone
without knowing someone will be there to meet me. AnandiMa
and Dileepji arranged for every detail of my travel to her *ashram*

in Nikora. I was met at the airport by a relative of Dileepji, and met at the train station in Bharuch by Vinodbhai, the *ashram* manager. Everything I needed at the *ashram* was provided for me. I had an apartment, could cook my own meals if I chose, although I mostly ate the communal *ashram* meals. Once I settled in, I began the preparation of the sanding of the bronze Guruji statue and the mixing of metal-based patina.

A-a-h, to be home again in the spiritual presence of Mother India and the guru's abode. I often meditated at dawn and dusk on the top floor of the marble *ashram* overlooking the Narmada River with the water buffalo wading in the river, the golden warm reddish light of the dawn bathing the scene, and opening my heart. This was the color I chose to paint Dhyanyogi's statue—the color of the shore of the Narmada River.

When I arrived at AnandiMa's *ashram* I was despairing, grieving, hopeful, and excited about a new life, expecting miracles. I was also like the prodigal daughter returning to my guru and spiritual motherland. I felt my guru's presence through the guru *tattva* come to offer me refuge and healing through the finishing of his memorial sculpture. The loving reception of my guru brothers and sisters at the *ashram* was a panacea from the loneliness and desperation I had been experiencing after leaving my marriage. I felt loved and secure that I would somehow be okay in my new life.

February 2009, Jasmina inside the *Sri Yantra Temple* before patina application on Sri Dhyanyogi Murti created by a local sculptor

Jasmina outside the *Sri Yantra Temple* applying the golden metallic patina to her bronze castings of Sri Dhyanyogi's hands and feet made in 1991.

Jasmina to the right of Sri Dhyanyogi Murti
with the new golden metallic patina

Four weeks later, I had finished my commission. A great celebration of many *sadhus*, disciples, and Hindu priests performed a Prana Pratistha to reinstall Guruji's *prana* into the statue. The statue then became enlivened with energetic presence as a blessing to all those who visit, pray, and meditate there.

I was looking forward to resting for a few days before returning home to Maine when I became gravely ill with e-coli. It's considered a great blessing to bathe in the Holy Narmada River. While bathing in the current fully clothed in my *Punjabi*, I couldn't help but notice the animal feces floating by. Within twenty-four hours, I woke at 1:00 AM with a fever, vomiting,

135

and unable to drink fluids. Blessedly, an American disciple doctor friend was able to help me with energy healing techniques so that I could keep down the Cipro medication I brought with me for such emergencies. The medication turned things around in two days, which kept me from staying in the local hospital miles away in Bharuch.

While recovering from the fever aches and dehydration, a local woman from the impoverished village with the most beautiful green eyes and dark brown skin, saw me lying on my bed from the bedroom window. We often would smile at each other as I walked the *ashram* grounds. Seeing my suffering, she came in my room and held me while I cried in her arms like a baby. Her love went beyond the need for the understanding of words that neither one of us could offer. As I write this, I send you my love, beautiful woman, wherever you are in the village. I am impressed by the dignity and courage the village women of India have without all the material security we have in the U.S. Many of the village women raise families with little food, in a hut without running water and the comforts we take for granted. We in America are accustomed to material comfort and always want more, yet we often lack the spiritual and psychological self-esteem and strength of the village women of India.

Outwardly, my marriage was over, my financial security gone, and my health threatened. I had lost everything that I valued in my life. What did I have to lose now? I am free to go anywhere and do anything. When things get so bad, there is nothing else to do but look up—do or die. Have you ever experienced that, beloved reader? Then you know what I mean. In India, I reestablished my strength in the Inner Guru guidance, faith, trust, and courage.

I returned from my India sojourn in March, 2009. At my Guru's Nikora *ashram*, I worked in the beautiful *Sri Yantra*

*Temple* and stayed in comfortable *ashram* surroundings with my meals provided. Now, I was getting free food from the local food pantry. Funny how fate can have you living in a marble palace one week and shopping for free food handouts the next. As the saints say, "It shouldn't matter feast or famine." I did have to remind myself, though, while standing in the snow and ice in line for the food pantry to open—to feel gratitude for the free food, and feel the camaraderie of my fellow shoppers. I was even able to get organic produce.

For the first week of my return to Maine from my five-week stay at the Nikora Ashram, I was on Indian time. On the second night of my return, I awoke at 2:00 AM restless and ready to go. But where? I put on my coat, hat, scarf, and winter boots to brave the raging snowstorm and bitter early morning cold and wind. The door to the outside stairs wouldn't budge with the snow leaning on it. I kicked it until it opened, and found my way to the car I hadn't driven in five weeks. It sputtered to life and took me to the destination I hadn't been in years since the brain tumor recovery days—my sculpture studio.

I found the key I kept hidden under the doorframe. The door opened to my workspace just as I left it years ago, although basement dust and cobwebs cluttered the space. There was the wastebasket full of trash from my last project. And there was the sculpture in wax of the divine mother in the form of the great yogi saint Sri AnandamayiMa that I had abandoned, waiting for my return. During this time, I started sculpting again—finding my creative impulse to return to my love of manifesting form.

# 36. More Miracles

$M$y newfound freedom, although scary to me because of all the uncertainty and the survival worries, was an exhilarating kind of stress that gave me the bravery, uncoupled from my marriage, to create a new life on my own. My divorce proceedings were going well, thanks to my lawyer who provided a very discounted rate for her services. In April, I left for South America to receive my miracle healing.

What can I say about an experience beyond words, beyond the mind—into the realm of miracles? It is our birthright to ask of the Divine whatever it is we want. I wanted it all—my tumor completely healed, a beloved partner to share my life, my finances restored, and success in my healing practice and art. I literally brought it all to surrender to the spiritual beings working through the master healer.

Did I get my desires fulfilled? Yes. But not all at once. I had to wait, reaffirm trust, and do my own healing work to let the miracle do its work on me. Sometimes, one can be healed and not cured or cured and not healed. There is no blame in sickness. The ultimate healing is for the physical body to die and for our soul to return to the spiritual planes of existence. Our spirit is immortal. I suggest if you have doubt about that to take up your own explorations into the spiritual sciences. That said, the fear of dying underlies all of our fears.

Years ago while waiting in my chiropractor's office, still very much in recovery from the brain surgery, I overheard the conversation of two patients---one to the other about a friend with cancer. They discussed her illness with a judgmental attitude. They agreed, "She wouldn't have cancer if she took better care of herself."

Even saints get sick. I have known plenty of folks that meditated, ate the best diet, exercised, and still got sick. Sickness is a call to go deeper into the core of our divine connection. The clearing from the body, mind, and spirit that illness can bring is a fast track to an elevated state of unconditional love. To be around a sick person is to be in the presence of the divine call to love. It is a holy circumstance and a gift to the patient and the caregiver.

By the time I had returned from the first trip to the healing center in South America, I had noticed that the slight partial paralysis left over from my surgery years ago, noticeable only to me when climbing stairs, was gone. I experienced emotional healing as part of the process of clearing sickness from the body. Every disease has its counterpart in the spiritual energy body and eventually makes its way into the physical. It can take years to grow a tumor.

I had this dream: *The master healer calls me onto a stage that is surrounded by people. I am standing on the stage with the healer, who takes a rough kitchen knife and slices my abdomen open. Out fall hundreds of worms, onto the stage, crawling over the edge. "Don't go near them," I say to the large crowd around the stage.* The dream was telling me the spiritual cause was operated on and released.

In another dream, I saw my mother as a young, happy, vibrant woman in a beautiful green dress—the woman I never saw as a child or adult. She was modeling her dress for me. I saw her in her innocence, her wholeness for the first time in my life. *She is not her mental illness any more than I am my brain tumor.* The mother wounds to my soul were healed, along with my perception of my mother. To this day, my mother and I have a more authentic, accepting, and caring relationship, with healthy boundaries.

*Om Parama Prema Rupaya Namaha*

Cosmic Vibration of Creation! Attract the highest form of Divine Love into my Life!

# 37. I know You're Out There Somewhere...

*I* went home from South America in April 2009 feeling healed of the tumor and ready to attract the beloved who was out there somewhere. Before I left, I was told by the master healer's guides to expect the blessing of finding my beloved mate anytime after returning to Maine.

Three weeks later, I received e-mail from E-Harmony online dating service. I have never gotten one before. At first I thought, *No way.* Then I thought. *Well, maybe God is giving me an opportunity to meet my beloved.* Since I didn't know where my beloved was, I intuitively knew he was not in Maine; I decided to cast my anchor to the world. Sure enough, things started to move in that direction.

If any of you folks do online dating—I advise you to be honest about who you are and what you want. There is someone for everyone out there. I wanted to share my spiritual values with a similar partner. I had many matches but I knew in my heart he was the one when I saw his photo, along with the honesty and integrity in the answers to my questions. I felt the kind, healing energy in his eyes asking me to reach out to him.

We started e-mailing, then phone calls. In July, he came out to Maine from California to meet me. He won my heart from the start. Kenny is his name. He got out of the car, presented me with a dozen yellow roses, and bowed. A spark ignited in my heart. I knew for sure he was the answer to the prayer. I just had to give it time.

Our first weekend together was short and sweet. Neither one of us wanted to become overwhelmed with the other, yet secretly wondering and hopefully knowing, will we part as friends or lovers? Or both?

On our first night together, he tucked me in bed, read to me a beautiful spiritually inspiring passage from his favorite book, kissed me goodnight on the forehead, and slept on the living room sofa bed. It felt pure and sweet—my little girl within felt secure and safe.

On the second night, I decided to test him. "Okay, I said. "Let's sleep together as friends." I stretched out next to him. He reached for my hand and gently held it. I felt something I have never felt before with anyone else. It felt like his hand was my hand, like I was holding my own hand. For the first time since the guilt and trauma of leaving my marriage, I felt my own purity and innocence. We were two divine children at play in the sandbox of life. On the third night, we were ready to become more than friends...for that; you will just have to imagine the rest, dear reader.

When we fall "in love," it is not illusion. We see the qualities of that particular person's higher self that attracted us in the first place. In living our day-to-day life, we can start to overidentify with the human aspect of our loved one. We can fail to see the miracle of our beloved. Maintaining the miracle connection to that special person is the conscious work of each partner.

In Kenny, I recognized his purity of heart, his gentleness, his humor. That's a big one for me in my former life, which was desperately in need of a sense of humor. He was emotionally and financially stable and deeply committed to his own spiritual growth. Another big one for me. We had a lot in common. We both had to recover from brain injuries. He was in a coma as a young man after surviving a car accident, which required him to be in rehab for six months. He majored in sculpture in college, as did I. We both had profound connections to the spirituality of India. For the first time in my life, I could be with a man who could offer me safety, security, adventure, and a love that we could grow together.

Right away, we started to know each other, and that included the shadow side. We got down to the business of that really fast. It doesn't mean a new relationship is doomed to fail because we start to see the flaws. The flaws are there to draw us closer together by healing the masculine and feminine wounds we all carry. We decided to give our relationship a chance.

# 38. Esperanza (Hope)

*August 2009*

*I*an and I came to Kenny's home near the ocean for a week visit at the end of our vacation visiting friends and traveling down the Big Sur coastline. The first thing I saw was the full seven-foot jasmine bush surrounding the length of the house. I thought, *That's me, Jasmina, named after the flower, a symbol of beauty and purity.* Sheltered behind the bush, Kenny's home revealed it's rustic presence with weathered brown wooden shingles and green trim. It looked like a simple single family home you would expect to come upon in the Maine woods. This charming rustic home triggered a deja-vu reaction.

We walked up the fern-bordered stone steps to receive the welcoming smile and embrace of Esperanza, Kenny's housekeeper. The warmth of her smile and embrace reassured me *everything is going to be okay here.* The beauty of Esperanza's warm, brown eyes, the ocean air, the scent of jasmine was a gift from an earthly paradise I had been secretly longing for a very long time. *Yes, it is possible to be at peace, to be whole and healed in such a place.*

"Mister Kenny has been waiting for you. He is so excited you are here." Kenny came to meet us at the door, his face beaming with happiness as he handed me the keys to his house. This was a special key with a beautiful red rose painted on a white background. The red rose is my favorite flower.

As I crossed the threshold of his home, came a bigger surprise.... *Now I understand the deja-vu reaction.* Several years ago, while I was still in my former marriage, my husband and I planned to build a house on our property. The house I had envisioned was a rich dark brown with wood shingles and green trim. When I stepped inside the living room of Kenny's home, there was the vision of the dream house from years ago—a large field stone hearth that led into the kitchen. The placement of the other rooms was the same. Little did I know that the house of my vision was the one I would have in another location with a different partner several years down the road.

I came to know and love Esperanza, her story and life as a refugee from El Salvador. She was a tiny, slender woman with long, black, wavy hair, warm sparkling eyes that have suffered much, yet full of joy, hope, and courage. As a young woman of nineteen years, she escaped with her infant in her arms from the war-torn country. Thirty years later, with tears in her eyes, she told me about the terror of living in the city with the sound of gunfire and bombs and the one that took her brother's life while he was working in the fields.

Esperanza was not embittered by her past—just grateful for her life in America and the love of her surviving relatives. She was deeply spiritual and full of enthusiasm as she lovingly organized and cleaned our home. She became my confidante, my heart compass pointing me in the direction of accepting love, having hope and faith in the new life I was creating, always reassuring me, "Mister Kenny does love you very much."

Sadly, she was not to be with us for much longer; yet, she was with us long enough for us to never forget her influence in our life. In May of 2011, just two months before our wedding, she died from a massive stroke. As we said goodbye the last time we saw her alive, she was thrilled that we were to be married. In lieu of her physical presence, her family attended our wedding. To this day, I gather spiritual strength from her presence in my heart.

At the end of our two weeks in Kenny's home, we then decided to move in together. I quickly went back to Maine.

Things seemed to be moving so fast in my relationship with Kenny. My friends were even wondering if it was wise to be making this decision so soon. "You hardly know each other." It felt right to me. Even so, I wanted some sign from my spirit it *really* was.

One afternoon after washing my dishes, I turned and noticed a small sparkling symbol on the rug by the red couch. I knelt to pick it up. It was a beautiful silver paper cutout of a six-pointed star. Where did it come from? There all by itself. Aha! That's the message from spirit!

Kenny and I in some ways are worlds apart. He grew up in affluence. I grew up in survival mode. He was Jewish and I Christian with a strong mystical connection to Christ. We joke about this. I am a HindChrist and he a HindJew. The six-pointed star on my rug was the Jewish symbol of wholeness. Yes! I am reclaiming the Jewish connection of lifetimes ago. I am coming home in this relationship.

In September, I quickly closed my coaching practice with the medical center. Kenny came out to help me move. At the end of September, from there we went to the Omega Institute for more healing sessions with the master healer. I thought the tumor was healed on the first trip several months ago.

What happened? A month after returning from South America in April, I had a follow up MRI to the previous one I had a year and a half ago, which revealed the tumor had started to grow back. This latest MRI revealed the tiny lentil sized tumor was slightly larger than the last one. *What do you think? Do you think the healing didn't work? Or maybe the tumor stopped growing and the growth happened before the healing?*

I had to hold all the anxiety thoughts in neutral. I didn't know. I still needed to be in a place of hope to keep my healing energy going. I did know that I needed to go back to the master healer and continue my healing.

When he saw me at Omega, he told me to return to his healing center, saying, "Come as soon as you can and I will take care of it for you when you get there." I went back to settle in with Kenny in Los Angeles. Six weeks later, I returned to South America beyond hope, expecting more miracles to unfold.

On my first day at the center on our tour of the grounds, we came to the spiritual surgery room. The door was wide open. It's supposed to always be closed unless the master healer is in session. The energy for healing needs to be maintained. It was eerie seeing the door wide opened. We were advised to just look in, not enter. I looked in and had that spooked feeling—like the room was waiting for someone. The maca surgery recovery bed was against the wall.

We sat outside the surgery room on benches listening to our guides give an introductory talk. As I was listening, I saw a beam of light from a portrait of King Solomon streaming out of the eyes and the frame—a white bluish light—it came towards me. Just before I passed out, I shouted out to my tour guides, "I'm having a surgery. Brain tumor." I then passed out and fell into the lap of an energy healer, Alex, who was on our tour to receive healing for a health condition. To the left of me was an emergency medicine physician from the U.S.

I am retelling this to you from my memory and the testimony of the witnesses. The medical doctor could see a being of light attached to me. I had passed out from the effects of the spiritual anesthesia, as if it was regular medical anesthesia. I have often smelled it as I passed by the spiritual surgery recovery room when the master healer was in session. It smelled just like the good old anesthesia I have become so familiar with from the many operations since childhood. I could hear voices but I could not talk as I lay passed out on Alex's lap. My arms and limbs were paralyzed. The medical intuitive, Alex, could see inside my head, to an orb of light operating on the tumor—he could feel the heat coming out of the old surgery drill holes from the 2001 surgery. The EM doctor monitored my pulse, noting it was thready and faint under the effects of the anesthesia.

Alex told the crowd gathered around me not to move me because I was being operated on. Another medical doctor who happened to be on the grounds monitored my condition. The maca bed was wheeled out of the surgery room. It was me the surgery room was waiting for.

My guides informed me later that energetically, the room was prepared knowing I was coming. And the master healer did say, "I'll take care of it when you come to the center." I lay on the maca bed in the surgery room for an hour...in and out of consciousness, hearing sounds and watching scenes unfold of a lifetime thousands of years ago during the reign of King Solomon. In this emotionally laden scene I was re-living the original cause of the brain tumor growing in this life. I was a man—short, very muscular, wearing sandals, clothed in a brown rough cloth, wielding an ax in the midst of a battle. The details of what happened in that battle are not clear. An axe blow to the head? Or did I give one? Whatever happened didn't matter. I knew the root of the beginning seed of the emotional trauma was pulled out. Eventually, I was carried to my room at the *posada* and lay on my bed for an hour and a half, at which time I was fully recovered and walked to lunch.

On that trip, I stayed for three weeks to continue healing on all levels. My desire to have the many fibroid tumors on my uterus healed took second place because the brain tumor diagnosis was more life-threatening. I did receive healing for the fibroids but they were not to be healed until a year later. The healing spirits who work through the healer see the totality of the cause of the illness, which can be quite complex as its roots extend into the emotional and mental energy fields.

151

I made a vow before I left that I would go back one more time to make a Jesus statue in gratitude for the healings. A Jesus statue to someday have enlarged, cast in bronze, and installed at a special healing center to be determined in the U.S. May that intention be blessed in abundance to bear fruit in due time.

Before I left South America, I was shown in a dream the house and garden I would live and sculpt in when I returned to the healing center. Sure enough, after almost giving up and ready to sign a contract with a real estate agent for another property, I was introduced by a friend to another homeowner's property — the one I saw in my dream. I sometimes wonder how many times we are mysteriously guided and we don't hear and don't see because we are not paying attention?

Before returning to Los Angeles, I met Kenny in Australia to go on a silent retreat with his spiritual master. I had another one of those messages from Spirit in a most unexpected, extraordinary way.

## December 2009.

I am shopping at a dollar store outside of Melbourne, Australia in the small mountain village of Kallista. My fiancé, the clerk, and myself are the only people in the old time store.... The discount shirt looks like a good buy for $10.00. I feel a slight electrical sensation on my skin. And I turn to face a woman, a stranger standing a foot away. She looks at me and speaks as if she were expecting to meet with me. She seems to know everything about me. In a clear, firm voice, she says the name of the well-known master healer I was with in South America three weeks ago. "I have a message for you! Spirit wants you to bring your message of healing to the world. And be real about how hard it has been for you. Spirit will guide you and is waiting to speak through you." My sense of time and place collapses.

I am finally doing it now, beloved reader. Am I being real enough about the challenges? I hope so. Somehow, words are not enough because the transformation in spiritual healing is beyond language. Silence is the closest language to convey it. Words are all we have until we evolve enough to do it through silence.

*Jesus with Sacred Heart,* 7-inch bronze statue by Jasmina Agrillo Scherr. The bloodstone (mystical Christ stone) heart with diamond center and the garnet stigmata invite you to connect with your sacred heart within, to transform suffering into healing, peace, and joy.

Part Three

# Living in the Heart

# The Heart Sutra

*Gaté,*
*gaté,*
*paragaté,*
*parasamgaté.*
*Bodhi!*
*Svaha!*


Gone,
gone,
gone beyond,
gone beyond the beyond.
Awakened!
So be it!

# 39. My City of Angels

*I* returned to my beloved, new partner Kenny, rejuvenated, whole, and deeper in the healing process than ever before — living in my heart in the City of Angels. Adjusting to my new life was more of a challenge than I thought it would be. I started having flashbacks of memories of my life in Maine with my former husband and son, Ian. It seemed like everywhere I went, I was reminded of Maine — a street corner, a child's face, new friends — I was so easily triggered into nostalgia and grief. I became a haunted person.

Living in two worlds, the old and the new, drove me to seek help through a divorce recovery program in Santa Monica. The program helped me to come to terms with what worked and didn't work in the marriage. And then to let it go which was the forgiveness part. John and I had fulfilled our karmic destiny — our purpose, the crown of which was to parent our beautiful son, Ian. Not all relationships are meant to last a lifetime. Our family was not broken apart, but now broken open. I knew I was getting better when I could stay focused in my present circumstances. Even so, letting go of the past is a process over time, especially with divorce recovery.

Living in the heart doesn't mean a bad thing is never going to happen to me or that I am never going to be stressed out with the challenges life presents. It just means I am practicing making an honest, sincere attempt to grow in my spiritual intelligence and apply its intuitive guidance in my day-to-day life.

Kenny and I are growing in our commitment to love and share our life together and in service to others. We have our own path and yet join each other — separate, yet equal parts of our union becoming whole. In each other's eyes, we see the divine soul of ourselves and we see what is not whole — the shadows of ourselves that we need to own, embrace, to become even more whole. It's a continuation of the journey we have always been on and will continue to the next phase without a body — in the spiritual plane of existence. By the way, we did get married, on July 9, 2011, at the Self-Realization Fellowship Lake Shrine Temple in the Pacific Palisades — the very same place I wished upon decades ago on a cold winter night in Maine.

My city of angels, you are the western Mumbai of my life. You are alive with the full spectrum of the chaos of life in the fast lane — its creativity, spirituality, wealth, poverty, in living and dying. I know many miracles await me and challenges to go with it.

Jasmina and Kenny Agrillo Scherr married July 9, 2011, at Self-Realization *Lake Shrine Temple*, Los Angeles, Ca.

# 40. Betrayal

*I*n January 2012, a big shock shook my emotional world. A very close friend I recommended to go see the master healer, was raped by him. It turns out there are many, many, other women he has violated. When she returned in secret, literally in fear of her life, from South America, she was suicidal. As a spiritual sister, I was immediately at her side, to hold her close and affirm for her the beauty and dignity of her divine feminine being. I realized at the same time how emotionally traumatized and betrayed *I was*.

I was so afraid, filled with doubt that I feared to be alone with myself at our home without Kenny, who was away on a business trip. I was afraid the spiritual entities working through the master healer who I had opened myself and invited to help me heal would turn against me. As a very young child, I could see and feel auras and the presence of spirits. As I grow in the spiritual power of love, I perceive the veil between the physical world of our five senses and the unseen world of spirit reality. I am not talking allegorically here. Just as there are friendly and not so friendly people in our physical existence, there are actualized forms of consciousness (spirits) that have a positive and negative influence upon us through our thoughts and emotions. Because I was psychologically traumatized by my friend's rape, I was not able to offset with a positive state of mind negative influences from the spirit world. I stayed with my friend while her understanding husband provided safety and food for us.

I was so weakened by the betrayal I even felt separated from the spiritual connection in my heart and the intuitive guidance that first told me to see the healer in South America. *Was the healing real or not?* Dear reader friends, my passion for well-being got the best of me. I got angry at the fears. I would not accept it. Refused to accept it. You see, it's okay to get angry at our negative, habitual, turn on yourself emotions. I went deeper into my own wisdom connection. It's okay to get angry with God...go ahead.... shout...scream.... I cried, let myself grieve, and waited, letting the answers to the questions come over time.

I stayed with my friend for the first three days of her initial raw trauma. During that time, a doctor colleague from Maine e-mailed me, asking for a recommendation to the master healer for a relative with cancer. I was forced into coming up with a truthful, compassionate reply. What do you say to someone with the life-threatening challenge of cancer? I felt the urgency for me to come up with a truthful, compassionate reply. I must encourage faith, hope, and healing for them. I thought of the thousands of people who have experienced the miracle of healing through the healer and still are.... What do I say to that? Yet, if I don't tell the truth to expose what is truly wrong and criminal, I won't be able to sleep at night.

I got mad and requested to the Divine, "I want to know *NOW* how to reply to this letter!" And then I let it go and went to bed. I woke up the next morning after clearing some of the emotions with my heart practice, the answers coming in bits and pieces throughout the day. My understanding grew as I continued to work to spin clear the emotions from my heart and help my friend do the same. By day three, I was able to be alone in my home and write the letter of reply to the doctor friend.

Dear _____

*I wish there was no need to have to send a message like this....*
*As a person of integrity, I am contacting those who have been*
*connected to _____ through me and those who have*
*recommended him to me as well.*

*Although I have experienced healing from the physical to the emotional in having sessions with _____, I can no longer recommend folks going to him. A very close friend of mine was raped by _____ at his healing center. Luckily, she escaped, returned to the U.S., and is now working to heal from the sexual abuse. He has been sexually abusing women and possibly children in secret. You can research this by googling him as "sexual predator." This is very sad and of course morally wrong and a crime! I have an intuition that it is a matter of time and he will be publicly brought to justice.*

*Taking a spiritual perspective on this situation, the paradox is that spiritual healing and the opposite of that can exist side by side. We have spiritual healing ability we can develop through our own faith and love, aided by meditation, prayer, spiritual practice, heart connection, doing activities that bring a feeling of peace and joy, aided by our fellow healers of whatever healing modality we are attracted to help us in our goal of healing and happiness. My healing is happening as a result of all of these, along with conventional medical help as desired. This in no way negates the power we have inside – which is the miracle that happens when we apply the laws of love in our life.*

*Join me in saying a prayer for the healing of the many women and children who he has abused, for the protection of the folks who are sexually vulnerable who come to _____ for healing, and of course, for the healing _____needs, and that the public be informed.*

*In Love, Faith, and Miracles,*
*Jasmina*

Two weeks later, I was emotionally healed enough to send a copy of the letter to anyone I had a connection with through the healer. As I emailed the letters I felt my own fears in the wake of taking a stand to warn others—the fears that I would be abandoned by my friends in the healers' community; that people would distrust my recommendations and guidance in the future. I had to face it and offer it to the divine by getting real all the way to universal source.

After I sent the letter out, I heard the still small voice of my heart say, *The letter is going to have far more effect than you can imagine. Your signed name on the letter has the vibration of purity and truth.* How can one e-mail letter have such an impact? Well, it did. It went around the world into the healer's hand and contributed to him not being able to come to the U.S. to do healings for two years. The circulation of the letter around the world alerted some women who could be vulnerable to sexual assault at the healer's hands. Is my heart hardened? What did I learn? You may have your own wisdom on this...and why did I go there in the first place?

My spirit guided me to learn to hold a high enough spiritual vibration to be open to the healing pouring in from the universe—to be open to receiving rainfalls of healing light. And secondly, to be so strong in the healing vibration, I was able simultaneously to file out the evil going on there, and receive miracle healing from the entities working through the master healer. It reminds me of the story I read over twenty years ago, about the concentration camp guard assisting people into the gas chambers—knowing they were going to their deaths. She did not want them to die in a state of fear—but to be in the light as they approached death. The reports were of her counseling the inmates, illuminated in light. She was a comfort to those she assisted to their deaths.

A paradox? Yes. In my youth, I felt appalled by this. How could she assist them to their deaths and comfort them at the same time? Now I know. Yes, it can be so. Can you hold the paradox that *good and evil can exist side by side* in your heart like a

Zen *koan*? Can miracle healing and violation be going on in the same place? Yes, it can at our physical reality. We must be so strong in holding the light of love in the midst of the greatest evils—even if we cannot entirely stop the evil. We can do our part. And it matters. Every drop of love matters. Has an effect that will bear fruit in its time.

The betrayal was an important reminder to me of an important lesson in spiritual maturity. Spiritual enlightenment is different than having spiritual powers or siddhis. Someone can be a channel for miraculous healing powers and still commit the crime of rape. Likewise, someone can be in the highest states of unconditional love (enlightenment) and not have miraculous powers. Having siddhis can be a great ego distraction from the goal of becoming a fully integrated human being illuminated in the light of love. In the end we are called to be true to the Divine Intelligence operating in our own hearts. What is healing if not the call to be in a state of unconditional love—which is to be in a state of equanimity, in compassion, forgiveness, and joy in body, mind, and spirit.

# 41. 2012 and Beyond....

$I$ call 2012 the year of the naked truth globally and personally. This was the year of rapid change, chaos, and eruption affecting everyone. Yet, beneath the ruble in the breakdown of the old familiar structures in our relationships and in our living conditions, a new order of shared loving and living that includes a deeper care for ourselves and the earth is happening within our intimate circle of loved ones and the global family. In our shared vulnerability, we have the opportunity to come together in compassion and compromise to recreate a new way of being in service to each other.

As a memoir is just one person's story of unfoldment in the cosmic plan to realize and live day-to-day the deeper truths of living in peace and joy, yet each story makes up the whole. The only life we can live is our own. I am coming full circle once again in my life....

It has been more than three years since my divorce. I have started a new life and marriage to Kenny; yet I cannot put my former husband out of my heart. Our hearts don't care who was right or wrong. Our spiritual heart loves anyway in spite of our judgments. It has been my daily spiritual practice to send forgiveness and well wishes to him and myself. It has been my daily practice to be honest in the admittance of my reactions to lovingly embrace the lingering guilt feelings, and grief and ask through prayer and meditation for the feelings to be replaced with compassion and understanding. Asking always provides relief as I continue to heal emotionally.

One of the miracles of the after effects of the divorce is that I have been able to rebuild a more loving relationship with my son. Children suffer greatly in divorce. Ian felt betrayed, angered, and hurt, and acted that out with me. I made a conscious decision to deal with my own reactions to his behavior privately and to do my best to put him first, to let him know I loved him even though he was hurt and angry with me. I am so glad I never gave up on having a relationship with him. We have had many fun adventures in his visits to California. I am enjoying getting to know him as the extraordinary wise young man he is becoming.

## *July 2012*

I usually check in with Ian by phone every few days. He just returned to Maine from a three-week visit at our home in L.A.

"Ian, how is everything going getting back into life at home?"

"Mama, I have something to tell you about Papa." His voice sounds distressed. "He...I just found out. I wish I had more time since coming back to deal with this. Papa...has...throat cancer."

I am shocked into silence. "What are the doctors saying?"

"The doctors say they have caught it in time in an early enough stage to treat it. They don't want to operate because it would be messy. So he is going to have intensive radiation and chemotherapy treatments. But first he has to have his molars removed to prepare for the radiation treatments."

"I want you to know I am here for you. I love you and I care about Papa. I wish for his health and happiness. He is in my prayers. I am praying for his complete healing and support from the community."

For days, I felt lost in a sea of grief and mixed emotions. Did my leaving the marriage stress him out so much he got cancer? I know that is a childish thought but still, I couldn't help thinking it.... My intuitive guidance from spirit told me that this experience of suffering was as much a part of his spiritual growth as my brain tumor healing was for me. I am not to blame. It couldn't have been avoided.

I felt compassion for the suffering that would be part of John's healing. I wanted to be able to take care of him as he took care of me in my healing from the brain surgery over a decade ago. Yet, it was not my place anymore. *I could focus on my son's needs. I could function as a spiritual healer through prayer and meditation. That would require that I rise to a level of unconditional love detached enough to go beyond my own emotional reactions.* My daily practice of sending heart intention of healing helped me cope and to listen and coach Ian through his own process of coming to terms with living with his Dad's diagnosis, to function at school and enjoy his favorite activities.

Over the next several months, I felt a spiritual grace descend, elevating me to a level of emotional detachment to not overly identify with the suffering of my former husband. In honor of my own grief, I needed to withdraw from social activities. During this time, I began the creative project of this book. At first, I thought, *How can I begin such a project during a critical healing crisis in my family? How could I not? There is never a best time to begin. The time is now!*

## *Nov. 19, 2012, Westbrook, Maine.*

Kenny and I visit Ian and his dad at their home in Maine. As we walk up the driveway in the cool late fall air, I fast track to the memories of the hurt, blame, and noncommunication of the divorce years. I feel vulnerable. I pray to Spirit: *Dear God, guide me to not be controlling, to listen, to be present in the moment in a state of love and healing.* And I am grateful. I thank God for John's change of heart. This is the first time he has been open to having us come into the house and talk with him.

In my mind, I see the photo of him on Facebook with our son, taken during his cancer treatments. Ian told me the cancer tumor on his throat is gone. *Thank God the treatments are over.* In the photo, he looks rail thin—like someone who has been through hell and back. He lost his hair—his once muscular body looked shrunken, wasted, and frail, his posture stooped over. He is smiling, though, with proud joy at our son's scholastic award.

I ring the doorbell. I am prepared. I take a full breath and let it out slow and easy. Even so, I am still a little nervous.

Ian greets us with a smile that is also a little unsure but welcoming. "It's okay to see Papa." There he is sitting in the living room in the red floral comfort chair that was my Christmas present many years ago.

"Is it okay to sit and talk with you?"

"Yes."

He looks better than the photo. Still very thin and weak—but his aura is lighter, more expanded. I see the auras of persons who are soon to leave the body as having a tint that is like the night sky. Not the case here. His energy is coming back. The ordeal of suffering has purified him emotionally. The anger is gone. "I have no issues with you," he let me know when we talked on the phone a week earlier.

We chat about the aftereffects of his treatment and the healing ahead. He has "chemo brain." Chemotherapy and radiation injure the brain. I reassured him his brain would heal over time. That he is healing beautifully. Even though his brain intelligence has been compromised, his spiritual intelligence has grown. He is more clear, understanding, and compassionate. Empathetic emotions are starting to well up. I remember my own suffering and vulnerability.

He tells me the story of his financial debt at the hospital and cancer center that with his current state of disability he cannot ever pay back. He is one of the many Americans who could not afford to pay for health insurance. "They forgave all the money I owe. Any further treatments I may need are free of charge." His voice starts to choke in gratitude and tears well up in both our eyes. Ian has told me how the church community, relatives, friends, and former clients gave of their time and financial support to lift him up in this time of need.

Later at the Super 8 Motel, Ian and I chat over a fun competitive cribbage game. My son is a brilliant math and science whiz, but I am still the cribbage master! He shares how difficult it has been to see his dad suffer. He knows that his presence living with him is helping him heal. Then he says, "Through suffering, we gain spiritual wisdom."

As I spent a brief amount of time with my former husband, in no way do I feel we are becoming friends, nor do I expect to; yet, becoming more communicative is a better way to put it. That is a small miracle seed we can build on. And as Ian grows through his college years, our communication will become more essential with regard to Ian's guidance. As it is best for each of us in this trinity to remain positive, uplifting, heartfelt, and clear with what is really happening.

It is now almost four years I have been living in the City of Angels. Living in such a vast sea of like-minded folks, I have been able to integrate who I am as a multidimensional being in my past, present, and future spiritual selves. I am free to identify with the traditions of being Gnostic-Christian, Jewish, Hindu, Buddhist, New Age, and so on... at one time or other, I have been all of them. In L.A., I can be the healer, writer, artist, beloved wife and mother. Yet, I am not any of those traditions or roles. I am just me. Who I am.

Healing is an inside job that extends over lifetimes. We are multidimensional beings living within the speed of light in the now—past, present, and future. Whether the healing happens physically, emotionally, mentally or spiritually, it goes on and on after the death of the physical body. Quantum physics, the spiritual traditions, my out-of-body light experience in recovery, and my meditation experiences indicate this.

I am still healing. I live with the uncertainty of brain tumor diagnosis on a day-to-day basis. I have chosen to not constantly be checking with an MRI unless intuitively guided to do so. I need to keep my energy high to live in the now, which is all we have anyway. Over the last year, the fibroid tumors large and small that covered my uterus are now gone. I take full responsibility for my well-being in the holistic sense through right living in food/supplements, exercise, prayer/meditation, and using my talents to serve others. Yet, even the greatest of saints get sick. There is no guilt or blame, just a call to keep on loving in the moment.

I live within the paradox that death is the final healing, can happen anytime, yet passionately on a daily basis, renew my intention of bringing in healing light of peace and joy and to consciously remind myself to be that light to all I come into contact with. I want to remain in this body as long as I can. I also at times catch myself worrying and getting stressed at the small stuff. I remember someone visiting me when I was bedridden during acute brain surgery recovery. He was very stressed about the looming bankruptcy situation in his life. In my debilitated condition, I thought that was obscene. I remind myself not to sweat the small stuff, as I transform the ongoing challenges in daily living, reaffirming I have achieved mastery in the soul lessons I came to affirm for the world.

The biggest miracles are the ones that happen that we don't see as physical proof. Does the state of love end? No. Not in this body or out of this body. The frequency bands of love go on and on. Through our heart, we can connect with the spiritual emotions of care, compassion, appreciation, joy, peace, forgiveness...this immediate now connection brings in enlightened moments. The secret to spiritual evolution is one enlightened moment after another. And the secret to heaven on earth is one enlightened action after another.

One of our greatest challenges is this: We must develop the *will* to notice when we are not in the frequency bands of love. Ah. That's the practice. To catch ourselves and to reconnect to our spiritual guidance, knowing how to be love in this moment, this place, this time, with whoever and whatever our circumstances. Whenever we apply the laws of love — gratitude, compassion, peace, forgiveness, we change the reality of our experience, in the moment, in the past, present, and future simultaneously. Can you just imagine how it is going to save our planet? We can create new world upon world in the newness of love.

# The Retreat House

So I am going to allure her,
lead her once more into the desert,
where I can speak to her tenderly.

~ Hosea 2:16

# 42. Soul Secrets: A Multidimensional Invitation

*January 2013.* I have come full circle once again. I await the next stage in the ascension of my soul's growth spiral. There is nothing I have to do to bring it on. It will happen naturally. Even so, I am not completely comfortable in the in-between. I live in an aura of expectancy.

*February 2013.* I am inspired by the subtleties of winter in Southern California. The cool wind blowing in from the ocean creeps up over the canyon, bringing layers of fog and mist, and with it, a sense of awe and mystery that settles itself into my expectancy.

Although we live in the city of L.A., our backyard is a canyon with its own ecosystem. I often awake at three AM to hooting owls, a pack of coyotes yipping through the canyon. By day, the deer freely roam, even to the large window in the back of our bungalow. They know we love them and will not harm them.

On this night, I tuck myself in early at ten PM. Before I sink into the oblivion of sleep, I breathe a prayer of forgiveness, gratitude, and protection to my angelic guides, letting the intention soothe and smooth my heart's rhythms into the peace of slumber. I sleep deeply. For hours. Then, from the deep forgetfulness that sleep brings, I am aware of my place on our bed, asleep, fully aware I am in astral dreamtime.

I find myself at the Encinitas Hermitage in Sri Yoganandas' receiving room. His living quarters have remained as he left them upon his Maha Samadhi in 1952. The rooms are roped off and are a special blessing to the spiritual pilgrim who views them. I observed when I visited on retreat last October; the rooms still bear his astral imprint.

In this astral dreamtime, the rooms are not roped off, but in full use by the myriads of people coming and going. In the receiving room, other astral realities are intersecting from all directions. Frame upon frames of rooms unfolding from my life, yet others' as well, like a cosmic grand central station. Many people are coming and going around me. They are in their own world of purpose. We do not take notice of each other.

I stand in the middle of the room. Of a sudden, Paramahansa Yogananda appears in front of me. He looks younger than the photos I have seen of him before his Maha Samadhi. He is wearing the dark suit he wore to address the multitudes when he was embodied on earth. His eyes are intense—the energy flowing out like lasers locking onto my eyes.

With his eyes locked on mine, he waves three shiny black stones in front of the middle of my forehead (third eye chakra). I feel an electrical shock wave. I see a large, single, beautiful, royal blue eye rimmed in gold. I start to fall back. Yogananda catches me.

"I am supporting you and will help you to lie down," he says as he gently and effortlessly guides me to lay on the rug. I open my eyes in bliss to find I am back on my bed, my husband sleeping beside me. It's 4:00 AM. *Let me go back into bliss.* I fall back into a deep sleep. After wakening, I am walking on clouds of bliss for several days as I go about my activities.

I take walks around the old sycamore tree sheltered sidewalks in our fairytale like quaint neighborhood, pondering the meaning of the astral experience. Perhaps a blessing—an opening to a deeper level of soul realization? A calling to new vistas? A part of me doesn't want change, instead wanting everything to remain the same. After all, I have been through so much already—best leave well enough alone. What brought this blessing on?

I reminisce how after living in L.A. for several months when I moved from Maine in 2009, a friend said to me, "Do you know that you are living very close to the Yogananda Self-Realization Lake Shrine Temple?"

"I am?"

"You're practically next door! They have the most beautiful gardens around the lake. You are living right next to paradise. Do you know how lucky you are? If it were me, I'd be there every day meditating."

I am jolted by the memory surfacing...me in the gold-tattered chair in Westbrook, Maine, reading *Autobiography of a Yogi*...decades ago... wishing I could be at the Lake Shrine Windmill Chapel. At the time, I thought the wish was so unrealistic that I never thought about it again.

After my friend's pronouncement, I started going to their meditation services. The first time on the grounds, I became enamored by the beauty and the spiritual energy. When I entered the Sanctuary, I wept when I saw the photos of Christ and Krishna—which to me symbolized my integration of eastern and western spirituality. Here I can be at home. I am not split in two—the two are one.

*Beloved reader, every desire is accumulated in the subtle spiritual dimensions—to either manifest or be cancelled out through a higher calling. When the fruit of the desire is ripe enough, it manifests, although it may take a long time.*

*March 13.* I have been planning this meeting for several months with Brother Satyananda, the senior monk at the Lake Shrine Self-

Realization Fellowship. There is such a thing as divine timing and it's here at last.

Such a beautiful sunny, yet cool temperature day for this timely meeting. Long ago in the early Hollywood days, the Lake Shrine, known then as the Santa Ynez Canyon, used to be a silent movie film site. The large basin was naturally converted from the many springs in the area, creating the oval-shaped lake known as Lake Santa Ynez, the only naturally fed lake in all of L.A.

As you journey around the lake path, sheltered by the flower and plant-covered canyon, and soothed by the sound of the waterfalls, you are so entirely sheltered from city reality that no outside sounds penetrate as you meditate your walk around the lake. The Lake Shrine today is the City of Angels' oasis in the desert, where thousands flock to from all over the world. Since moving here from Maine where I lived near many lakes, this is where I go to soothe my lake-starved soul.

I wait on the bench in the courtyard, breathing in the flower scents, the beauty of the Lake Shrine with its swans gliding on the lake, the constant sound of the waterfall gushing from the foot of the large statue of Christ atop the cliffside. I have been going over what I think I want to say to Brother Satyananda. I brought my notebook to help me stay focused. I hope to come away from this meeting with some understanding about the spiritual transition I have been in for the last year. I chose Brother Satyananda after observing him interact with others and myself in casual spiritual topics of conversation. His lectures are inspiring and humbling. I sense this is a person of deep ongoing realization of the Divine.

Here he comes...across the courtyard, looking inconspicuously dressed in sweater/slacks ensemble, incognito in sunglasses. We greet each other acknowledging, finally getting to meet through the challenge of our busy schedules. We quickly decide to talk in the little glass–walled, octagonally shaped meeting room/porch on the courtyard.

Our little meeting room is small and cozy, with a cushion-lined wooden bench that I quickly choose, across from Brother Satyananda's chair. When he shuts the door to the outside world of the courtyard, I feel as if I am enclosed in a comfortable glass-enclosed time capsule. I am ready and alert to take off where our conversation goes.

Although I didn't choose the monk's spiritual path, I am curious to know how Brother Satyananda chose *his*. I am at ease to learn of his challenges in choosing an unfamiliar spiritual calling that required sacrifice and forgiveness from those he disappointed to follow his inner guidance. Like me, he has some past recall of former lives.

I am aware of my vulnerability at exposing so much that is in my heart. It's my confession to a witness of God. As Brother Satyananda listens to the unfolding of my life story—the intuitive sensitivities since childhood, my Catholic upbringing and mystical connection to Christ, and not fitting in with my birth family and other relevant details, my body is responding to something happening outside of my brain's being able to acknowledge.

My feet automatically shift to lay fully on the floor, and my hands of their own volition, to hold onto the cushion for support as I sit straighter and lean forward. Brother Satyananda is transforming in front of my eyes! His face appears to be a little more rounded and filled out...his eyes deeper, now brighter in color, are intensely gazing at me. There is more light around his head and it's flowing out of his eyes into mine. My memory is being tweaked.

Holly Jeeze! I am looking at Yogananda as he appeared to me several weeks ago in the astral dream. Brother Satyananda has merged his consciousness with his spiritual master—Yogananda!

Now, this little glass-enclosed octagonal room *really* is a multidimensional time capsule. I am a little dizzy from the shift.

I share the details of the astral dream. As I continue to hold onto my seat so that I don't fly off into spiritual space, Yogananda/Brother Satyananda further enhances my understanding.

"Yes." He acknowledges my interpretation of an opening and healing of the third eye karmas. "This was not a physical healing. The brain tumor was a result of karmas."

"Yes. In earlier lifetimes, I was a warrior. I don't feel the need to discuss this further." It is obvious to me he is peering into my soul and is seeing more about me than I am telling him. I am blessed by this.

As I discuss my former marriage, I don't need to provide a lot of the whys because the divine presence of Yogananda is ahead of me on the details. He leans forward to gaze most intensely.

"Beware of sentimentality!"

"What do you mean?"

"Looking back and pretending it was better than it was. This sentimentality habit can draw you back into the darkness between you. He hasn't learned from his illness in the same way you have. Your paths are meant to be separate. He has his path to God. You have yours. In your prayers, turn this over to God who is in charge.

"Also, beware of sentimentality in your family of origin. You are meant to be here, not over there with them. Pray for them all you want, but from here."

"For years, part of my spiritual practice of reciting mantras to clear negative karmas was to offer them to heal my families' lineage of depression and other addictions."

"You are helping them with that. But you cannot clear all of it."

I feel the compassion emanating from him with that statement. He is pulling out of me the last remaining seeds of sentimentality, over-responsibility, and guilt. I feel the pain of that in my heart and relief at having this taken away by divine decree.

We share a long moment of silence.

"A-a-h! And the book you are writing!" His face lights up with a smile as he leans back in his chair.

"What?!! I didn't mention my book to you! How do you know that?" I freeze in my seat and my breath stops. I have long hair. If it were short, it would be standing straight up on my head by now. As it was, every other hair on my body is sticking straight up, along with the goose bumps.

"I know." He nods with a playful hint of a glint in his eyes. I feel his mind going over the soul of the book without me telling him anything about it. "The book will keep you busy. It will find its way to the people who need to hear its message."

I share with him my *shaktipat* connection with Sri AnandiMa and Dhyanyogi, my spiritual progress throughout the years, and current spiritual practice. We chat about my *samadhi* experiences, the sacred Om sound that I hear in and outside of meditation, the little star of light that comes and goes in front of my eyes in meditation and in my daily activites. He is experiencing the connection and the bliss as I speak.

"Yes. Yes. Oh...but there is so much more. You don't need the *kriya* practices that involve intensive breathing as you have described. Your practice needs to be very subtle now. The *kriya* practice we teach is very subtle and will help stabilize you to go easily into deeper states of self-realization. You are invited to study the lessons and take *kriya* initiation in this path."

"I only want to go deeper into the light of oneness in God Consciousness. There is no longer any form to worship."

"That's what we do here. Give yourself time to think it over. In your meditations, ask permission of Dhyanyogi and God. Once you take the step of initiation into this *kriya* yoga lineage, you will be under the subtle guidance of Yogananda to reach your goal. It would be best not to mix other *kriya* yoga techniques with the *kriya* practice we will teach you."

"Within the guru *tattva*, all the Masters are one."

"Yes. It's okay to be in divine friendship with other paths and teachers." He was getting to the heart of what I was really asking.

"This is really between me and God and no one else. It's nobody else's business. So there really is no disloyalty." I honestly wasn't entirely sure of that, although I didn't voice it.

"Yes. That is true. I want you to still go through the process of asking permission to be sure. Take your time."

The Easter Candle in the Chapel of St. Andrew's Abbey

# 43. Starry Night

*T wo weeks later. Easter Retreat at St. Andrews Abbey, a Benedictine Monastery out in the desert of the San Gabriel Mountains.*

I am giving it time. Asking the question and receiving the answer. I take long walks in the desert hills. The answer is revealing itself. Divine wisdom answers through my heart. The heart channels its wisdom sometimes in a fast download of perceptions that I hear in my mind. Other times, it oozes its guidance as a feeling shift into a peace that calms me enough to "park it in my heart" till understanding comes, however long it takes.

In the process of waiting it out, I received the bonus of an intuitive download of understanding from my spirit.... *Who do you think brought you so near to the Lake Shrine when your soul called out decades ago? You were born with the desire to go to the fullest extent in realization of divine consciousness in this life. It is no accident you are here. Where you live now has the necessary vibration for you to complete your mission. The old you died in the brain tumor surgery. You asked for and were given a second chance. You got to keep the memories to aid you in fulfilling your soul's purpose. This is a new life. There is no disloyalty, no breaking of a vow. The time is ripe!*

And then one night came the astral dream that broke into my normal dreamtime sleep...Dhyanyogi appears in front of me—radiant in a white gown. He says to me: "These are the jewels that come from the brain in meditation."

I look down into a large glass jar in my hands. Inside is my brain. It is split open, its grey matter revealing deep within the center at the midline, three multifaceted, shimmering, deep purple stones.

I am in awe. Then I find that I am holding the stones in my hand. I am totally mystified. "Do you have these, too?" I say to him.

"Oh. Yes."

"Are these mine?"

"Yes. They are yours." I wake from the dream fully conscious on my bed.

I am letting myself live into the meaning of the dream—the symbolic associations of the stones, without overanalyzing. I know in my heart it's okay to proceed where this new initiation takes me. You, dear reader, are welcome to find the universal meaning in it.

## Good Friday

Out here in the spring desert climate at the Abbey, I am savoring the integration of my Christian and Hindu soul. I am savoring the opportunity to reenter the lessons of faith, trust, and surrender that suffering brings, as we walk and sing the prayers of Christ's passion through the Stations of the Cross in the desert hills. It's my passion, too. From deep within the tomb of my heart, I see into my private hell with the night vision of an owl. I bring into the light the lingering fear of a brain tumor diagnosis and the suffering of what I went through before and after the surgery. A fear of poverty. A fear of aging. A fear of dying a horrible painful death. A fear of failing in fulfilling my soul's purpose. My own cross to bear. I surrender into it all. I die to it all. And look to the resurrection of more love and light coming into my heart. All part of the journey. The sacred heart journey.

## Easter Vigil, March 30, 2013, Saturday

In this spiritual tradition, Easter is celebrated on the first Sunday after the full moon of the spring equinox. I have been looking forward to this special night all day, and made sure I was well rested in taking a nap. What a wonderful discovery and blessing this special monastery is to the pilgrim. The monks offer a hospitality that is kind, humble, and welcoming for folks of all faiths, with the added bonus of delicious food!

We wait until dark. At 9:00 PM, we proceed from the chapel to gather outside on the grass around the unlit hearth. We find our place in the utter blackness, with the moon and stars to guide us. The electricity in the entire monastery has been shut off to inspire our partaking of this ancient Christian ritual.

We are holding our unlit tapers. We share an easy camaraderie after two days of retreat silence. As fellow retreatants, our bond was born of silence. At first, it felt unnatural to be sharing the rooms and eating meals without speaking. Then, when it was time to break the silence, speaking felt unnatural. I noticed after the silence our communications were more from the heart—genuine and grateful.

I wait with anticipation for the mystery of what is to come. The cool desert night air is like a soft, gentle kiss on my skin. I look up at the stars in the clear dark sky. Then, an opening in our gathering is created as the monks now proceed out one by one. Father Luke steps out from the back of the procession, holding in both hands the four-foot unlit Easter Candle with its crown of bronze to hold the wick. This special candle represents the resurrected Christ, the anointed one.

Abbot Damien, in his white Easter garments, steps out to greet our congregation, and then proceeds to the hearth. He lights the fire of the central hearth that now represents Christ dispelling the darkness and blesses the flames.

185

Father Joseph brings the unlit Easter candle to the abbot, who carves on the candle a vertical line saying, "Christ yesterday and today." As he carves the horizontal line through the center of the vertical line, he says, "The beginning and end." At the top of the cross, he carves the Alpha symbol, at the bottom the Omega symbol, signifying that God (cosmic consciousness) through Christ (unconditional love) is the beginning and ending of all things.

In the upper left quadrant of the cross, he carves the number two, saying, "All time belongs to Him"; carves the zero in the upper right quadrant saying, "All the ages"; carves the one in the lower left quadrant saying, "To Him be glory and power"; carves the three in the lower right quadrant and finishes saying, "In every age and forever." Thus, representing our new year of resurrection.

One of the monks takes an unlit taper, lights it from the fire, and gives it to the abbot, who lights the unlit Easter candle. The lit taper has served its purpose—the abbot blows it out. Father Luke, proceeding with the lit Easter candle, stops at two designated spaces and chants, "Christ Our Light" and we respond, "Thanks be to God!"

In the dark, we follow the lighted Easter candle. After we respond the second time, "Thanks be to God!" the abbot takes an unlit taper and lights it from the Easter candle. He then passes it on to the next person, from one to the next, until all our candles are lit. Together, each in our own light proceed to the chapel to partake of the communion ritual of the eating of the bread (body) and drinking of the wine (blood) of the Christ Consciousness that is Unconditional Love re-awakened within us.

# Epilogue

At dusk, I sit on my chair facing northwest, overlooking the canyon with the nature sounds of nightfall lulling me into deeper meditations. I await the next level of initiation, to explore the universe in my own heart and the new vistas of multidimensional odysseys of my fellow travelers.

# The Gayatri Mantra

*Om Bhur Buvaha Svaha*
*Tat Savithur Varenyam*
*Bhargo Devasya Dheemahi*
*Dhiyo Yonaha Prachodayath*

Translation

Radiant Divine Soul from which we all came
Awaken the same brilliant Divine Light in me
So that inner radiance consumes all
thought and emotion
Teaching and guiding me to realizing reality

# Acknowledgments

$T$o first and foremost, my beloved husband, Kenny, your love and emotional support, for believing in me and holding me accountable to get focused to write and giving me the financial support to make the lifelong dream of the book a reality;

To David McArthur for the many years of skillfully coaching me using my heart's intelligence through very challenging life situations and reminding me "You've got to write the book!"

To Tom Bird, your soulful guidance and "author within" transmission permanently lit the flame of my divine voice and gave me confidence in that voice; To Rama Jon, for steering me through Tom's Publish Now Program.

Special thanks to the spiritual communities within the City of Angels:

To the Art of Living Family for renewing my spirit, faith, and trust that I can belong to the world family in L.A.;

To the Gnostic Center and Bishop Stephen Hoeller, for the blessing of baptism to a deeper commitment to living in the Light of Christ Consciousness;

To Healing in America, for deepening my ability to use the energy of light to give and receive healing for myself and others;

To the Self-Realization Fellowship for bringing me home;

To you my beloved readers, you are all so special to me. Without you, this book could never be. My gratitude is beyond words, even as words will have to suffice.

And last but not least, to all of you who have been my divine companions as I travel through life, blessing me with the lessons you taught me, including the hard ones. You live forever in my heart in love, beyond space and time.

# Resources to Lighten Your Journey

## 15 - 30 min. Mini Healing & Guidance Sessions with Jasmina

### Light Energy Transference
Experience Divine Light Transference to clear and infuse your entire body with light frequencies--bringing peace and healing at the cellular level.

### Divine Light Guidance
Every problem has a solution that is just right for you! Quickly access and use source energy to receive your highest intuitive answers on any issue.

**Visit** http://jasminaagrilloscherr.com/contact-me/ or call 310-230-8246 to schedule your mini-session on Skype or by Phone.

## Jasmina's Life Coaching Programs

### Resilience Training
Journey inward to discover your strength! Jasmina will help you emerge from crisis or trauma to recapture your balance and sense of joy. She'll work with you to find your hidden well of wisdom, self-love, capability and endurance. But there is more to resilience then bouncing back. It's creating the new *set-point* of happiness, inner peace and vitality. You'll experience once again, just how good life can be.

## Heart-Based Divorce Recovery

Why live with anger, bitterness, resentment, fear, or a lingering desire to return to an unhealthy situation? Jasmina will help you live for today and tomorrow, instead of the past. To let go of all the emotions that are interfering with you living a big-vision, happy, love-filled life today!

## Our Miracle Heart

Your heart is more than just a beating organism. It is a conduit to your higher self and source. It has its own intelligence, an intelligence that interacts with your consciousness, subtle energy system, physical health, and what you project into the world that manifest your experience. In learning how to connect with your heart, you will discover gifts you never knew existed! By looking to your heart, you will find answers, meaning, and purpose!

**Visit** www.jasminaagrilloscherr.com for a free consultation on Jasmina's life empowering Coaching programs and realize your next discovery.

# Guided Meditation CDs

- *Receive Intuitive Guidance From Your Divine Inner Light*
- *Receive Intuitive Guidance From the Sacred Heart of St. Francis*
- Visit http://www.shop.jasminaagrilloscherr.com/main.sc

# Jasmina in the Garden